SWEET AS CAN BE

Jan Frewer

SWEET
AS CAN BE

Jan Frewer

WYMER
PUBLISHING
Bedford, England

First published in 2023 by Wymer Publishing
Bedford, England www.wymerpublishing.co.uk Tel: 01234 326691
Wymer Publishing is a trading name of Wymer (UK) Ltd

Print edition (fully illustrated): **ISBN: 978-1-915246-20-2**

Edited by Jerry Bloom.

eBook formatting by Coinlea.

A catalogue record for this book is available from the British Library.

Typeset/Design by Andy Bishop / 1016 Sarpsborg
Cover design by 1016 Sarpsborg.

Contents

*You are all stars about to go
on an amazing journey*

Preface

Some time ago, I was listening to the radio and the DJ introduced a song from 1967. It was a novelty record called 'I Was Kaiser Bill's Batman' by Whistling Jack Smith. You may or may not have heard of it. Anyway, after he had introduced it, I remember thinking, "Well, that's nothing, I was Sweet's Sound Engineer!" Could that be a song I thought to myself? 'I was Sweet's soundman' by Mixing Jan Frewer!"

Probably not I concluded. But then I (call me crazy) have written a daily diary since I was given my first one on Christmas Day 1959, which was a Boot's scribbling diary for 1960. I started my diaries on January 1st 1960. It is now 2023 and I have never missed doing my bedtime diary in all that time — not a single day.

Suddenly it dawned on me that I had a mountain of material for a book. A book with a difference as this would be written from my perspective, touring the world with the band. I got quite excited by the idea.

To get to the beginnings of The Sweet and my time with them, I need to go back in time a little to the mid and late sixties. I was an amateur musician, playing bass guitar. I had my own band called Wainwright's Gentlemen.

Towards the end of this band's time, I wanted to change the lead guitarist. The guy I wanted, Robin Box, said he would join if the drummer from his band, Roger Hills, could also join. It seemed like a great idea, but when Mick Tucker moved on, Brian Connolly, by then, the lead singer decided to go with him, to form a new band — The Sweet.

Great decision, guys — best move you ever made — You cracked the big time!

You may find the sequence of reading this book unconventional, but I have never pretended that I am a novelist, or ever will be. My brain though is overloaded with the 1970s working with Sweet.

You will soon notice that things are not recorded in the order that they happened. The reason being I don't want you to feel that you are reading a detailed diary. A lot of what you read will be in the order that memories came flooding back to me instead of everything being in perfect order and specific sections, I have endeavoured to take your mind on a little rollercoaster ride, in some places, to add to the fabulous insanity of it all — big smiles for all coming up — I promise.

I just wanted to give you all, as much fun reading about my years as Sweet's sound engineer as I had working with the guys. Thank you all.

Thank goodness I kept my diaries. I was touring the world with the best band ever — The Sweet.

After England I lived in Lake Tahoe, California for many years, and I now live in Merida, Yucatan, Mexico. I am now 75 years young and have never missed a day of making a diary entry. Over 23,000 entries in that time. This is the most comprehensive and thorough account from this period and generation because it's from the inside. I sincerely hope you enjoy this book as much as I did writing it, after delving back into my memory.

Jan Frewer, July 2022.

Wainwright's Gentlemen

How did Wainwright's Gentleman come to be? I wanted a bigger more professional band where everyone would be going for the top. I became interested in music from right back to Elvis Presley days and Lonnie Donegan. My favourites were Elvis, Little Richard, Bill Haley and the Comets, Buddy Holly and the Crickets, Jerry Lee Lewis and Eddie Cochran.

Everything happening in the music world made me so want to be involved so I thought I had better buy a 6-string electric guitar which I almost did. But I spoke to a guy in my school… James Searle who had just bought a guitar because he liked the lead guitarist in The Shadows, namely Hank Marvin. He said that we should form a band and could I get a bass guitar which I did.

We had a drummer at our secondary school named Robert Kingsnorth and he had a friend called Steve Smith who wanted to play rhythm guitar. So off we went with just instrumentals at first because everyone was crazy about The Shadows. I then decided that I wanted to sing as well so we started doing our favourite vocal songs of the time.

I formed the band, Wainwright's Gentlemen in the early sixties and my dad was the manager (God rest his soul). He wasn't a musician but he worked as a supervisor for Kodak. He just wanted to help us and used to organise our gigs. He bought us an old yellow van to travel in. There were times when he had to leave work early to support us at gigs so his colleagues used to cover for him.

We did very well with lots of gigs being offered — it was a good time, that's for sure. Wainwright's Gentlemen played a lot of London clubs in 1964 and 1965. In early 1964 we were doing well with gigs in Middlesex and London. On the 9th January 1964 at the Hammersmith Palais there was an area competition and Wainwright's Gentlemen knocked out a band called The Detours who went on to become The Who. At the final on 6th February Wainwright's Gentlemen won the contest that night.

The Boyz at the ready

Over the years things changed and new faces appeared. Wainwright's Gentlemen was a west London band, most notable for containing several musicians who went on to fame and fortune in the late 1960s, early 1970s.

Not in special order, but members of Wainwright's Gentleman included Jim Searle, Robert Kingsworth, Philip Kenton, Chris Wayne (Wayne was his stage name), Alfred Fripp, Ann Cully, Tony Hall, Robin Box, Brian Connolly, Mick Tucker, Ian Gillan, Roger Hills, Dave Brogden (he was a saxophone player and shortly after he joined is when Ian Gillan joined) Gordon Fairminer and Frank Torpey. All wonderful people to have had the pleasure of working with.

Wainwright's Gentlemen are (from left) Chris Wright, Phil Kenton, Jan Frewer, Jim Searle and Alfred Fripp

A welcome fit for gentlemen

WAINWRIGHT'S GENTLEMEN, formerly Unit 4, had noisy support from coachloads of fans when they won their heat in a Beat contest at Hammersmith Palais on Thursday evening. The group, three of whom come from Harrow, now enter the hall finals on February 6. A win there would put them into the area finals of the contest.

The group of five has been together for 18 months, playing at youth clubs and socials, mainly in the Hayes, Harrow and Wembley areas. They have recently acquired a van to take £2,150 worth of instruments and amplifying equipment from job to job.

Among the clubs the group has appeared at are Erkenwells Youth Club, the Annunciation Youth Club, the John Bosco Youth Club in Wembley, the Hayes Beat Club (where they are resident band), and two London coffee lounges where they are the resident group.

Members

The group comprises Chris Wright (vocalist), of 87, Kynance - gardens, Stanmore, who is aged 17 and is still at school; Jan Frewer (bass guitarist), of 110, Imperial-drive, North Harrow, aged 16, also still at school; Jim Searle (lead guitarist) of 16, The Drive, North Harrow, 17, apprentice engineer; Alfred Fripp (rhythm guitarist), 114, The Greenway, Hayes, 17, apprentice mechanic; and Phil Kenton (drummer) of 14, Trevelyan - gardens, Willesden, also 17, who is in advertising.

Wainwright's Gentlemen intend living up to their name, wearing smart clothes on and off stage. Sketches have been prepared for a new uniform for the group—in plum red.

The Gentlemen prefer beat

A coachload of fans from Harrow went to Hammersmith Palais on Thursday night to see Wainwright's Gentlemen, three of whom come from Harrow, win their way through the half final of the national Beat Contest.

The panel of judges commented on the group's new stage wear — plum red suits made by a St. Anns-road tailor.

Chris Wright, of Stanmore, Jan Frewer and Jim Searle, of North Harrow, Alfred Fripp, of Hayes, and Phil Kenton, of Willesden, will now contest the area final on April 2 at Hammersmith

Five Perfect Gentlemen

by Barbara Denny

Left to right:—Chris Wright, Phil Kenton, Jan Frewer, Jimmy Searle and Alfred Fribb.

THEY are not quite there yet but they are going to be . . . . anyway the young man with an American accent who manages them is quite sure of that . . . five young men who are going to swing the Gate (Notting Hill variety) into the place held now by Mersey side. Formerly known as "Unit Four" when they were playing at the Bedsitters Club in Holland Park Avenue they have now changed their name to "Wainwrights' Gentlemen"

"Really elegant . . . but the noise is just as loud" says Manager John Scott, (who cannot explain his American accent as he is a Londoner but 'guesses it must be show business'!) He described the magenta suits and frilled white shirts which apparently are now calculated to 'send' the girls more than sweaters and jeans. The girls, incidentally are already there . . amazing though it may seem, about 200 of them,

all screaming, when the five boys won the recent Mecca Contest for pop groups at the Hammersmith Palais.

HITS ASSURED

Unlike the Beatles (whom they intend to oust), the Gentlemen do not write any of their own material but some is written for them by a young song writer called Denis Edwards . . . 'He will write all their hit songs in 1964" said John Scott, (no 'ifs' or 'perhaps' you'll note . . . its all treated as a matter of fact, say you're there and you're there!).

"And look out for the Blue Beat" he added. "The Blue Beat is hitting the Town right now, with the Mods."

Who are the young men? None has the name of Wainwright, the nearest is Chris Wright the handsome young vocalist who is said to draw in the girls , the others are Jan Frewer (bass guitar) who is sixteen, Jim Searle (lead guitar), Alfred Fribb (rhythm guitar) and Phil Kenton, seventeen, on drums.

"We're all ready for bookings at £60 a night and more, there's the

fan club and a team of typists sending out publicity material all over the place," said John Scott, patting his pocket where he had the tape of Blue Skies which the boys hope will 'cut their first disc' . . . not to mention that crowd of teenage screamers.

GOOD!

"How's its done?" I asked Mr. Scott.

"Hard work" he said.

"Do they have to be good?"

"No! "he was frankly scornful" . . it doesnt have anything to do with it! . . . " (But added hastily that these boys were good) "We're just in the groove now . . . we've got it all fixed, these kids are just going right in there by the Beatles and past them!"

Mr. Scott folded up his sazzy press book, made me a breezy transatlantic farewell and left, first presenting me with a free photo . . .

It all seems a matter of formula to this theorum the Wainwrights and Mr. Scott have written Q.E.D. (which when I was at school also meant Quite Easily Done . . . !)

GENTLEMEN THIRD

Wainwright's Gentlemen, the 'beat' group made up mainly of Harrow residents, entered a contest at Watford Town Hall on Sunday and came third.

In beat final

Wainwright's Gentlemen, the plum-suited beat group with three of its five members living locally, have won their way into the finals of a national beat contest. They will compete at the Lyceum Ballroom, London, on May 4.

Ian Gillan — yes that Ian Gillan. The one who went on to Deep Purple. Unbelievable really to look back and think of that time and how he became our lead vocalist along with a female singer Ann Cully (who I have never been able to trace in recent years). Mick Tucker incidentally was my drummer at this stage.

As time went on, as we know, changes happen and Ian left to join Episode 6 and of course from there Deep Purple. Ian was very professional with a great voice and very dedicated in the way he put his everything into the band and of course went on to a great future in Deep Purple with his fantastic voice and a great presence on stage.

We were busy for a few years at the start of the rock band scene. Great times were had by all, as we were all still working and doing gigs in the evening — and lots of them too.

I don't recall what my other band members did when they left school since my heart from day one was loaded with what I wanted to do, who I wanted to be, where I wanted to go and to be totally involved in what I really love — good music.

I was fortunate to have a great young manager, Norman Horan at my day job at Charles Philips Food Store (which became Tesco) in Rayner's Lane who wholeheartedly supported my musical ambitions and let me go early on nights when we had gigs. Thanks Norman!

My job was filling the shelves with food products and I wanted to help fill the world with wonderful music.

And many years later, hey presto, Sweet came and played a concert in the town where I lived (as you'll read later in the book).

Here's a funny little story about Wainwright's Gentlemen (not so funny for all):

Saturday 26th December 1964:
Star & Garter, Windsor, Middlesex.
We finished the gig and were on our way home in our yellow van, which sadly overheated, and we needed water.

We decided we had no other option but to knock on somebody's door and ask for help even though it was Christmas.

This we did, and to our surprise a vision that can only be described as 'Dickensian', came to our rescue. A man dressed in his striped pyjamas, dressing gown and also wearing a night cap (just like Wee Willy Winkie) opened the van door.

We obviously apologised profusely for disturbing him to which he replied, "no trouble boys I'm happy to help you". This was indeed a most charitable attitude, given that as he had opened the side door of the van, one of the band members 'who shall remain nameless' simultaneously leaned out of the van as the man leaned in and vomited all over his hairy dressing gown!

I think he must have liked rock bands!

****

The life of a musician is definitely not a traditional one as my first wife will attest…

On 28th August 1968 I got married, and at 12:30 the following day, Robin, Roger and I (having picked up Tony Hall on the way) took the 12:30 ferry from Dover to Ostend and embarked on a European Tour.

Our very first gig on 31st August was at Baumholder US Base (Germany). We did three spots that went down terribly badly because they only wanted soul music. They were about three years behind the times!

We followed up on 3rd and 4th September in Butzbach and on to Mannheim (Spinelli and Funari Barracks), This was followed up with numerous gigs in Munich and The Old Timer Club in Rüsselsheim which all went down a storm, returning to the UK on 7th November 1968.

NOTES

Repetoire.

(1) MORNING DEW
(2) SUMMERTIME BLUES.
(3) 634 - 5789
(4) WAIT TILL TOMORROW.
(5) ~~[struck through]~~
(6) OUTSIDE WOMAN BLUES
(7) ~~[struck through]~~
(8) ~~GIMME LITTLE SIGN~~
(9) ~~[struck through]~~
(10) HEY JOE
(11) FIRE
(12) ~~[struck through]~~
(13) GREAT BALLS OF FIRE
(14) BABY DONT YOU NEED A MAN LIKE ME.
(15) I NEED LOVE
(16) LADY MADONNA.
(17) MUSTANG SALLY
(18) RUNNING OUT
(19) LIKE WE USED TO BE
(20) ROBBIE'S BLUES
(21) CRY LIKE A BABY
(22) ~~[struck through]~~
(23) DESIFINADO
(24) EVERY LITTLE BIT HURTS
(25) GOOD TIMES
(26) BLUES IN B♭ (BLUE BASH)
(27) MY BABE
(28) ~~[struck through]~~
(29) HAPPY BIRTHDAY
(30) HUSH NOW.
(31) ~~[struck]~~ KIND OF LOVE IN
(32) READY TEDDY
(33) RIP IT UP
(34) HOUND DOG
(35) TUTTI FRUTTI.
(36) HARD TIMES
(37) DRIVIN' SOUTH
(38) SLIPPIN' & SLIDIN.
(39) STUMBLE
(40) WHY DONT YOU CHANGE YOUR WAYS
(41) PHOENIX.
(42) ~~[struck through]~~
(43) POINT OF NO RETURN
(44) FOXY LADY

This was our repertoire for 1968.

Beauty aids? Just part of the Sweet's stage make-up

FOR more than two hours before they go out on stage, the members of The Sweet are hard at work . . . applying lipstick, rouge, eye-shadow, beauty spots and powder.

For 'On the Scene's' cover boys this week, who have just leapt to the top of the charts with their new single "blockbuster," have the reputation of being the most glamorous of the new wave of "glam-rock bands.

And it's not just facial make-up either. Their usual stage gear includes silver boots, glitter trousers, red zipper suits and coats of many colours.

The boys admit that there have been times when their

By BOB STANTON

● The Sweet in some of their elaborate costume which the kids now expect. So what if they do get the occasional wolf whistle?

outrageous appearance has provoked the odd wolf whistle and shout of ridicule, but in general it's added to their appeal, they say.

Lead guitarist Andy Scott, comments: "We've really elaborated on the make-up and clothes and it has all got a bit out of hand. But the kids like it and expect it now."

Brian Connolly, the group's lead singer, adds: "We were wearing colourful make-up two years ago, long before anybody else. So we haven't jumped on a bandwagon or anything like that."

"Blockbuster," which starts with an electric siren, is the group's first Number One in Britain, although their previous singles have all done well here and they've had seven gold discs for sales in Europe.

There are some who have branded the band as just a commercial hit-making machine, who record other people's songs and get the maximum help musically from session men and producers.

The Sweet always emphatically defend themselves against such criticism.

"The argument about commercial pop being inferior is stupid," says Brian Connolly. "I think a hit single is the hardest thing to write and make. You've really got to know how to find that extra magic."

The group are also writing more and more of their own material, adds Brian, and he points out that, anyway, most of the B-sides of their hit records have been songs written by them.

Future plans for the group include an LP of rock songs dating back to the 1950's. The rock medley which they do on stage has always been a high point of their act.

At the moment, of course, they're basking in the sweet success of "Blockbuster" and the wave of fan mania they're stirring up all over the country.

GROUP FACTS

Lead singer: Brian Connolly, born October 5, 1949, in Hamilton, Scotland.
Lead guitar: Andy Scott, born January 1951, in Wrexham.
Bass: Steve Priest, born February 23, 1950, in Hayes, Middlx.
Drums: Mick Tucker, born July 17, 1947, in Hayes, Middlx.
THEIR SINGLES: "Funny, Funny," "Co Co," "Alexander Graham Bell," "Pappa Joe," "Little Willie," "Wigwam Bam" and "Blockbuster."
"Blockbuster," the group's first Number One in Britain, hit the top spot only two weeks after it was released.

Steve Priest: ' I don't have to prove I'm a man."

Steve minces his way to the bank

FOR a married man with a four-year-old daughter to chase the title of the prettiest boy in Britain, is surely the gimmick of all gimmicks—even in the pop world.

But Steve Priest, 25-year-old bass guitarist with the chart-topping group The Sweet, who uses make-up, false eye-lashes and lipstick in the cause of his art, rides the gibes of "raving pouff" . . . and minces all the way to the bank.

"I don't give a damn what people think," said Steve at the studio where the group are making their new single disc, Hellraiser. "The girl fans love it. They say it turns them on.

"And if the fellers in the audience resent that we look prettier than a lot of the girls they're with — well, they still seem to buy our discs.

"Another form of jea-lousy is in the pop scene itself. There aren't many girl singers today who look up to much, and they get mad because the comparison with us strips 'em of what little glamour they have got.

"We don't have to prove that we're mascu-line. People who pro-test too much about anything begin to look suspect.

"My wife, Pat, regards it all in the same way an actor's wife would if her old man was playing Charley's Aunt.

"And Lisa, my young daughter, has a good giggle."

Living On The Sweet Side Of Life

To get into my book, this is the first thing that happened with The Sweet — let me tell you:

Tuesday 27th March 1973: Sweet at Oaken Gates Town Hall. After the concert we all went back to my house in Shropshire, England. The guys said they had gigs lined up and needed an out-front sound guy and asked if I would be interested. I said yes.

Saturday 31st March 1973: My wife and I drove from our home in Shropshire to my parent's home in Staines in Middlesex. In the evening we went to Dunstable to see Sweet perform. Very impressive... really great material and with a lot of energy from all the band members. I was getting very excited at this point. My wife and I brought Brian home as we were staying nearby at my parent's house. His wife Marylin came back too, and it was the first time I had seen her in five years — lovely lady. At this point I had no idea how much my life would change. At the time I had a used car business and a carpet fitting company. Great... but... I wanted something different.

I think when you have music ingrained into you, you just cannot let it go. Everything started to happen very quickly. I was introduced to the other members of the roadcrew, Terry Price; Terry's cousin Ian Martin who was always known at Cuz, and John Wayte — only ever known as Bruno. Great guys. Very different to the everyday way of life guys. You cannot be normal in the rock music business. The good thing was, we all got on well from day one and attuned ourselves to each other, with a mission to make Sweet huge stars and us the Super Crew. So... on we go.

Life on the road can be very demanding, and that applies to the whole team. It would be rather boring without dramas, upsets and anything else that came along. Seventy-five per cent of the time is like a wonderful roller coaster ride with every moment, something crazily good happening and getting better.

From this point on, more started to happen every day. A great surge of new fans, which may well include some of you reading this book right now. It was a very uplifting point for all connected with Sweet. From here the escalation point was incredible. They were updating all their sound equipment, their amplifiers, in fact pretty much everything. We all knew that this was going to be big and successful, and an exciting time for the band, the management, stage crew, sound engineer (I was ecstatic), lighting team, and a lovely couple who were designing their stage clothes. I forget their names but I bizarrely bumped into one of them working in a ski shop on Mammoth Mountain in California when I was there skiing in the late 1990s/early 2000s. Just the atmosphere of it all was amazing.

Tuesday 3rd April 1973: Mick Tucker phoned me to say I have the job as Mixer/Soundman for the band. The rest is history — read on.

****

There are going to be a host of snippets as you progress through this book. Here comes one as an example:

Saturday 14th April 1973: My dad took Brian and I, and Brian's neighbour Philip — a doctor, to Penton Hook Marina near Staines to look at boats for sale. Brian and Philip bought a £10,500 boat they liked, (no small change then, a lot of money — over £140,000 at 2022 prices).

My God did we have fun in that boat over the next couple of years. We went all the way from Staines on the River Thames to the English Channel and back amongst other fun trips. The name of the boat was *'Francis Lee'*. This led to Andy buying a boat sometime later. It was a great way to relax for two busy band members. England was on everyone's minds at this time. The English fans had

SWEET AND SOUR (OR THE ROAD TO SUCCESS)

STEVE Priest, Andy Scott, Brian Connolly and Mick Tucker teamed up in 1970 unaware that just round the corner was a gold disc . . .

"We travelled all round the country. There is no better way for a group to get themselves known than to perform regularly. We realise now the money was low and the gigs second-rate, but our efforts

POP SPOT

by
DAVE CARTER

certainly paid off," said Steve.

To-day one of their singles is chirping away in the charts in Belgium, Germany, Holland and Finland. Another is climbing the American top twenty scale for the first time.

You may have guessed by now that the group in question are The Sweet who play Hanley's Heavy Steam Machine on Friday.

Listening to the "B" sides of the singles you might think The Sweet are heavy and hard.

On the top side—sugary and commercial, despite the rocky beat.

An explanation is that The Sweet's big break came when they met two gentle-

Blockbusting group The Sweet appear in Hanley on Friday . . . and return to the Potteries in June.

men named Nicky Chinn and Mike Chapman who wrote "Funny Funny", the group's first big hit, "Co-Co," "Alexander Graham Bell," "Poppa Joe" and "Little Willy."

Massive tour

They provided The Sweet with a formula that has helped them tour Europe and win both a silver and a gold disc. Total sales of the group's records are round the five million mark.

In June, the five-years-old band launch a massive British tour and are booked again for Hanley late in the month.

The man most people associate with the group is 24-years-old vocalist Brian Connolly, who was singing sweetly at the age of nine. When he was 12, he appeared on the box in a talent contest.

Incidentally, he was kicked out of Harrow Technical College for lack of attendance. He joined the League of Gentlemen, then the Generation before joining Mick Tucker with Wainwright's Gentlemen.

In 1969, The Sweet (as we now know them) were formed and released their first disc, "Slow Motion."

SWEET SUCCESS

ONE of Britain's leading pop groups, The Sweet (above) top the bill at the Baths Hall Scunthorpe, tonight for the second time within a year.

The Sweet first entered the British record charts early in 1971 with such songs as "Funny Funny" and "Co-Co."

As their fame gradually began to spread overseas the group had follow up successes with "Alexander Graham Bell" and "Poppa Joe."

But their biggest hit record came this year when "Blockbuster" soared to number one in the charts.

"Blockbuster" was something a little different for the group as it was the first sign of their attempt to get away from their early bouncy "pop" sounds to something a little heavier.

The group comprise drummer Mike Tucker and base guitarist Steve Priest both of Middlesex, lead vocalist Brian Connolly of Hamilton in Scotland and guitarist Andy Scott of Wrexham.

Their arrival in Scunthorpe comes just after the end of a tour of New Zealand and Hongkong.

At present they are in the process of recording a follow up single to "Blockbuster' and their first rock album.

to have something new, different, exciting and most importantly, great music. This, Sweet had in abundance.

The guys were all spending any spare time writing songs, which up to this time were being used as B-sides for their singles. Not their ideal choice but with big hits being written by Chinn and Chapman, they were very wise and went along with songs they knew would be huge hits such as 'Ballroom Blitz' and 'Blockbuster'. There would be plenty of time later to be in control of the A-sides, and of course albums. They were writing some amazing stuff to include on the albums. Everything was comfortable at this time.

The first recording studio the band were going to use after I joined the team was Audio International, situated in Baker's Mews just off Baker Street in London.

I just want to add a little bit of fun here. When I had my own band we were also the backing band for Gordon Waller of Peter and Gordon fame. One day in 1968, my guitarist Robin Box and I visited Gordon in Baker's Mews (where he lived) to decide which songs he would be singing on his next UK tour. Whilst we were there the doorbell rang and Gordon went to answer it…

He came back into the lounge with Paul McCartney! What a lovely guy, so modest. He told us he had just arrived back from India and a meeting with the Maharishi. As you can imagine it was an inspiring moment to meet 'my favourite Beatle'.

Monday 9th April 1970: I went and picked Brian up from his home and headed to London. He had a lot of calls to make. These included MAM, the agency that was managing them at the time, Tony Barrow's publicity office, and RCA records (for reasons I cannot remember, possibly to discuss switching labels) as the following year RCA became their label. We headed back and I dropped Brian off at his home. I went home and later in the day, my wife and I went back to Brian's house, where we had a Chinese takeaway — a lovely meal and a lovely evening was had by all. As you can imagine it was very interesting to watch Brian Connelly performing on stage from out front on the mixing desk, and also privately enjoying good times as a friend.

Security guards keep the fans at bay.

Roped exits no danger says concert tent owner

Exit doors were roped up for part of a pop concert at St. Ives attended by hundreds of teenagers, who had come to see The Sweet pop group.

The concert had already been running for more than half an hour and about 500 people were in the hall when a reporter pointed out the situation to security guards. The guards hurriedly undid the ropes. Later the owner of the tented dome where the concert was being held said the doors were never tied.

When the situation was mentioned to the organiser, Mr. Ron Broughall, he conferred with a security guard and said: "It appears there are ropes on the doors, but there is a steward on each one to whip off the rope if anything happens."

Three doors

It is believed that the doors were roped to prevent anyone getting into the dome during the night.

Of the six exits visible to the audience, at least three doors were tied with rope, one was partially blocked by group equipment, and another by a metal crash barrier to keep the audience off the stage.

The large "grand entrance" was clear.

The owner of the dome, Mr. Robert Fossett, said: "There is some rope over the doors, but it isn't tied up. There is a steward on every door and if anything happens they could be out straight away.

"Every bit of the dome is fireproofed — even the floor has been treated."

The hall is made of a fabric skin stretched over a metal frame.

Estimates for the audience at the concert, held on land near the Manchester Arms pub, Needingworth Road, varied from 800 to Mr. Fossett's guess of 2,000.

Easy exit

A spokesman for Huntingdon and Peterborough Fire Brigade's fire prevention department said on Tuesday that roping exits while people were watching entertainment was against the law.

"There must be a large number of exits available to people in this sort of thing, and it sounds as if there were enough exists but they just weren't readily available," he added.

"You should virtually be able to lean against one of these exists and be able to get out. To rope them up is illegal."

The spokesman said the tented dome had been examined by fire prevention officers, but obviously the door had not been roped up at that time. "Otherwise we would have objected."

No trouble

Extra police were drafted in from mid-Anglia towns for the pop concert, but fears there might be trouble from fans proved groundless. The final damper came when a cloudburst hit the site minutes before the music finished.

Mr. Broughall said: "The crowd is not as big as we had hoped, but then we had restricted publicity because everyone thought it might get out of hand.

"I am glad that the crowd have shown that they can behave, and that the fears were groundless."

Even one of The Sweet commented when he got up on to the stage: "There isn't many of them, is there."

The top pop group were supposed to have arrived in a helicopter, but in fact they slipped almost unnoticed into the grounds in a large black car.

The helicopter had been laid on in case large crowds gathered in the concert field awaiting their arrival, but only a handful of fans saw them come in. Most were inside listening to a supporting discotheque.

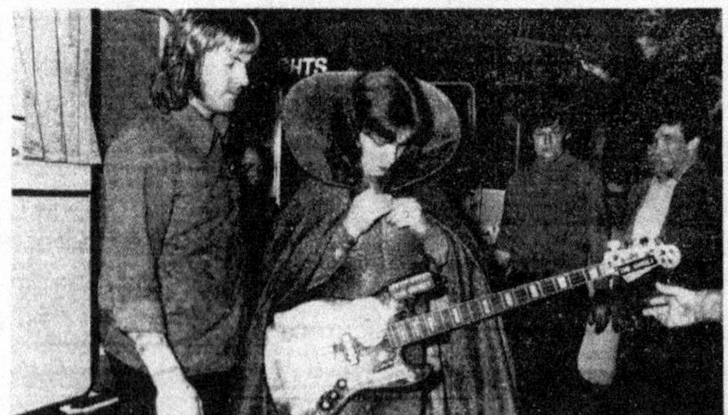

Steve Priest of The Sweet makes final adjustments to his cape before going on stage.

'BALLROOM BLITZ' IS TOP RECORD

"Ballroom Blitz," by Sweet, heads the *Melody Maker* list of best selling records this week, after being 15th last ewek. "Angel Fingers" by Wizzard, top last week, drops to second place.

Other placings, with last week's in brackets, are: 3 (10) "Monster Mash," Bobby Pickett and the Crypt Kickers; 4 (2) "Rock On," David Essex; 5 (26) "Eye Level," Simon Park Orchestra; 6 (3) "Angie," Rolling Stones; 7 (5) "Oh No, Not My Baby," Rod Stewart; 8 (6) "Young Love," Donny Osmond; 9 (8) "Spanish Eyes," Al Martino; 10 (20) "Joybringer," Manfred Mann's Earthband.

The singles and albums were doing well, so let's go touring for a while. My first gig as sound engineer with the band, was in England in Newcastle on 17th May 1973. We had rehearsed prior to this, familiarising myself with the beautiful Midas mixing desk. I felt very honoured I have to say, to be the guy out front giving the audience an incredible sound experience from the band. It was a tingle down the back experience as they gathered on the stage and put forward an amazing show to everyone's delight. Was I a happy bunny at the end of the show, to have been involved is such a great new experience? From being on stage in my previous band Wainwright's Gentlemen to making sure I hit the correct buttons to deliver their sound. I was very fussy, as the band were.

I am not going to comment on too many gigs as my main aim is for you to enjoy everything else that happened, the fun, amazing times and moments. Let's go forward to 1976 for a moment. We had finished a concert at the Mary E Sawyer auditorium in La Crosse, Wisconsin in the USA, and had loaded a giant semi-truck with all the sound equipment and were heading in our luxury camper vehicle to the Riverside Theatre in Milwaukee.

We were taking turns to drive the camper. Well, I was stopped for speeding and had to return a few miles to the police station to pay a fine. The officer wished me a happy birthday after reading my driving license! We eventually made it to Milwaukee with two more stops by the police but no more fines as both times the police said

The Sweet was their favourite band — pure luck. Hmmm!

Just two days later we were in the crew bus heading for Dallas. After 240 miles we had a tyre blowout. We had a second-hand tyre fitted and made it to the gig in time. After many gigs we headed home to England on March 25th.

Friday August 26th 1976: Flew to Tokyo via Moscow. Thirteen hours on the plane. Checked in to the Hilton Hotel on Saturday, had a meal, looked round the shops, chatted with Steve Priest and management and then went for a Korean meal. Gathered the rest of the band and went to the Biblon Club. Left at 4:20am and returned to hotel, showered and went to bed at 5:10am after being up for 28 hours with just four hours sleep on the plane, yet didn't feel tired. Probably would if I did it now.

Back to some of the things when not touring: One of the most amazing or perhaps nicest things to happen was on the morning of Monday 4th July 1978 (my Mum's birthday incidentally!). We were staying at a Howard Johnson's hotel right on the ocean front in Biloxi, Mississippi. It was fairly early in the morning and I decided to take a walk along the ocean front. I asked at reception for the nicest way to head. The receptionist said to go left as there was a big storm coming from that direction and I would be able to gauge when to turn around and come back. This I did. It certainly was a big storm and after a while I strode quickly back to the hotel. As I got to the entrance with a large swinging door, a gentleman approached from the other direction from the ocean front. I said, "After you" and he said, "No, after you!" It was then that I realised that he was Alice Cooper, who was headlining that night with Eddie Money, Louisiana's LeRoux, along with the Sweet, making up the four-band special evening. We had a little chat. Lovely guy. Totally unassuming. That night he was the Alice Cooper — Totally wild and exciting, being lapped up by the audience.

The Guys

Regarding the guys – they were all really nice in their own ways. They all obviously had their moments, some more than others. But we all have our moments, don't we?

Brian was one of life's genuinely nice guys. He was a true gentleman, nothing was too much bother for him, he was very polite, fun to be with, and of course a great vocalist with a very different voice of his own. Brian was one of those guys who wanted to be happy whoever he was socialising with. Despite his fame and fortune and possibly since we went back a very long way, Brian always went out of his way for me and my family and had a great relationship with my Mum and Dad. Brian was very modest and never showed any disregard for anybody. More later in the book.

Andy: Before life got crazy, I sometimes spent time out with Andy. Sometimes went to his house, met his family, listened to some of the song ideas etc. Very pleasurable. He often asked me to get bits and pieces for him… such as new loudspeakers for his home and anything really that he thought might be worth having, to push the band further into their popularity. Andy was a driving force within the band and was passionate about the band's future success. As we all know Andy is still performing to this very day… and still makes a great job of it to keep all the fans happy. More later in the book.

Now Steve was very unassuming, and a delight to sit and chat with. He knew where he was and where it was going and was quite happy with it all. A nicer bloke you couldn't meet. Everybody loved Steve of course, and quite naturally, as he was so laid back. He had a great sense of humour, never caused any mayhem and went along at the right pace with a good attitude. Steve never rocked the boat or expressed strong opinions unless really necessary. He was a super guy.

Mick had been the drummer in Wainwright's Gentlemen at the same time as Brian was vocalist. I was pleased to have had one of the best drummer's around, and he only got better and better as the years went by.

All the band members had ideas about which way the band should be going, Mick was up there at all times wanting to see Sweet get a bigger and bigger fan base and it paid off! Whenever they were seen in concert or on TV, hammering away on the drums behind the rest of the band, Mick was sending great vibrations through all of them.

Without the technology of today they were surging ahead purely on the strength of their music and their personalities. More about the guys later.

Recording Studios

Of course hundreds of hours were spent in the recording studios. These times can be very mixed — excuse the pun! If things are going well, everyone is on a high. If they are not it can be very stressful. I have to say about 90% of the time spent recording was dynamic with everyone on a Go! Go! mode.

At the beginning of Sweet's success, Nikki Chin and Mike Chapman were very influential with a lot of the early hits being written by them, and a great deal of the production of these songs being carried out by them, particularly Mike Chapman. I think these were happy times with one hit after another. As happens with most bands as time and years went on, the band wanted to produce themselves. More about that later.

They always had about three crew members with them in the recording studios. I always went because it was totally my bag seeing and hearing the construction of the ideas, sounds, changes, etc, etc. One of us would pop out and get food, they were very devoted to what they were doing and did not like to break off very often. Mine, and I think their favourite studio was Townhouse Studios. These studios were built by Sir Richard Branson in 1978 as part of the Virgin Studios group.

Before I forget, I must put this bit in... One late evening, after the band and everyone working their balls off to get a track how they wanted it to be, Louie Austin, the lovely guy who engineered a lot of their music, took a moment to… wait for it… everyone was crashing out, tired, having a nice drink or two — and Lou decided to have a bit of fun.

He found an eerie piece of music and played it in the control room but played it on the front mounted speakers and back of control room mounted speakers (as in Quadraphonic) and whirled this music around from speaker to speaker. All of us grown men (having enjoyed some delicious mushrooms earlier) nearly shit ourselves and couldn't understand what was going on. We ended up laughing and saying to Lou, "You bastard" a hilarious moment that I will never forget… Nice one Louie.

****

The Who's Who supporting the band.

Nicky Chinn- Manager
Mike Chapman- Manager
Phil Wainman- Recording Studio Sound Engineer
Louie Austin- Studio Engineer
David Walker- Sweet's Manager
Ed Leffler- Sweet's American Manager
Christine Bick- Sweet's secretary
Melody Howard- Sweet's secretary
Nico Ramsden- Extra guitarist, some tours
Gary Moberly- Keyboard player, Australian Tour

People

Well, the number of people you come across in this game, as you can imagine is huge. I am going to list some here, people from all walks of life:

David Walker (Handle Artists Management)
David was a guy I saw quite often and got on well with. As I see it, he did a great deal for the band and believed in them immensely. Every time I had to go to the office in London, I would say hi to David if he was there and end up in some constructive conversation. Sadly he passed away at the age of 57. R.I.P David.

I want to say at this point that looking back on all my diaries, because of overload of stuff going on, I was not able (obviously) to put everything into my diaries every night. What I hope I am achieving here is to give all my best, exciting, thoughts and memories to everybody out there.

Bang Martin (Martin Nicholas)
Now here we had a character... A really lovely way-out guy, absolutely full of ideas. He was the special effects guy for *Entec Lighting* who were based in Wembley, Middlesex at that time.

He always did a great job with any special effects, but I am sure you are wondering why he became known as Bang Martin.

I don't remember the details, but all I know is he had to create a loud bang during or at the end of one of Sweet's songs. This particular gig was coming to its end, when there was a truly huge bang which frightened everyone. Luckily no one was hurt in the incident. So he became 'Bang Martin' to us for ever after.

****

Going back to nearer the beginning, the band needed management suitable for what was coming fast. Lindsay Brown and David Walker was their management team in the UK and later, Ed Lefler was taken on as their manager for the United States.

Songwriters for the first few monster single hits were Mike Chapman and Nicky Chinn. (The band always had their own material on the B-sides)

There was a large London office for this purpose, helped along by Christine Bick and Melody who were both "super cool" secretaries. I still message and talk to Christine.

Louie Austin was the sound technician during this wonderful period, being well in control of the sound and mixing in the recording studio. The road crew were always there too, just in case anything was needed because of any technical problems with the band's equipment.

A few years later the band took the studio sound technician status on their own and believe me they played and recorded like magic. Deep down they always wanted to do this, but went along as requested, which gave them more time to write way more songs and think of performances and what would make all the audiences go crazy with the love of the band and their music. They wanted to be different and they were and way ahead of their time.

At this stage everything was happening exponentially with more and more success, on vinyl and on stage.

A group of people who put 'The Sweet' on the road. The four members of the band, Andy Scott, Brian Connelly, Mick Tucker and Steve Priest, are in the centre of picture. Also pictured is fan club secretary Christine Wood (back row, third from left). Front row includes roadies Terry Price, John Wayte, Ian Martin and sound mixer Jan Frewer. 8th October 1973.

DISCO TAKES

Three No. 1 singles made 1973 a very good year for The Sweet, but "Teenage Rampage" confirms my feeling that they may have to work a lot harder to repeat the success in 1974. The attack is similar on their New Year offering, fast and frantic, but the words get lost in some electronic gimmicks and the sound of the rampage. Even the essential easy rhyming catch lines now seem a bit too corny (RCA).

The fresh-faced youngsters of the Bay City Rollers could be one of the threats to The Sweet's teen market. "Remember" packs a catchy melody, a steady beat that should go down well at ballrooms and discos, and the words are simple and sung clearly enough to pick up quickly (Bell).

Alice Cooper has never been a consistently big singles seller here but "Teenage Lament '74" is a good choice 45 from his "Muscle Of Love" album. A steady pounding beat and a straightforward lyric saga of acne and young bewilderment with life with none of the Cooper horrifics (Warner Bros.).

They call themselves Three Man Army, and as they pound and shout their way through "Polecat Woman" the re-named Gun group lay down enough noise and action for a regiment. They keep the excitement high throughout a lively rocker that should get plenty of disco plays (Reprise).

"Hello It's Me" sings Todd Rundgren and if you can live through the rather plodding intro you'll find he does a good job on a catchy number with some clever backing harmonies (Bearsville).

It's hard to imagine a version of "Jackson" to equal that of Nancy Sinatra and Lee Hazlewood. Johnny Cash and wife June Carter manage it, however, with Cash's familiar twang well suited to the song and good timing bringing the most out of the lyrics (CBS).

FOR TEEN AND TWENTIES

Tailor made songs

Mike Chapman and Nicky Chinn may not be another Rodgers and Hammerstein partnership but they certainly know how to write a pop song that is tailor-made for a particular singer or group. The Sweet are climbing the charts with the pair's "Teenage Rampage," and the duo have also produced potential top three numbers for Mud and Suzi Quatro. A pounding drum intro lets you know just what to expect on Mud's "Tiger Feet" and what follows is the hard driving mixture of steady beat and simple lyrics that gave them a hit with "Dynamite." Not quite as catchy as their last single, it should still climb high (Rak)...

"Devil Gate Drive" finds leather lady Suzi re-creating all her previous hit sounds. The drummer again sets a racing pace, Suzi switches between her two pitches of roaring vocal, and a chorus adds the extra body. Very commercial and typical Chapman and Chinn material (Rak)...

Average White Band sound anything but as they produce a soft soul sound that belies their Scottish ancestry. "How Can You Go Home" is the title and it's a string-backed smoothie (MCA)...

"I Guess I'll Miss That Man," a flowing little ballad from the musical "Pippin," should re-establish The Supremes. It's not a great song, just pleasant, but Jean Terrell comes

Mike Chapman and Nicky Chinn.

DISCO TAKES

over well with a subdued lead and there are plenty of the familiar high-pitched backing harmonies (Tamla)...

Although it is sure to get plenty of TV plays as her new signature tune, I can't see much disco playing for "Baby We Can't Go Wrong" by Cilla Black. A gentle little ballad sung in the subdued style of the familiar nasal sound, but hardly a classic despite its "please join in" feeling (EMI)...

MUSICBOX

THE SWEET . . . new single out.

For the past three years, the New Year has begun with a hit record from The Sweet.

In 1971 it was "Funny, Funny"; 1972 was heralded with "Poppa Joe"; and 1973 arrived with "Blockbuster".

Can The Sweet maintain their record and make it four years in a 'row? They try today (Friday) with the release of their latest single, "Teenage Rampage".

The new single also marks the beginning of a new contract with their recording company RCA, and continued the group's association with their writers, Nicky Chinn and Mike Chapman, and producer Phil Wainman.

The Sweet pioneered the British teenybopper sound with their hits like "Funny Funny" and "Coco", but this year they successfully transformed their style to a heavier, so tougher sound which is heard to full effect on "Teenage Rampage".

8 EVENING MAIL SUPER STARS SPECIAL

March 1974

The line-up...Brian Connolly, Mick Tucker, Andy Scott and Steve Priest...not all paradise

by Jenny Heron

SWEET MUST DO IT THEIR WAY

IT is not easy to be a successful singles band.

But once you've reached that much-vaunted position, it is not always the paradise it's made out to be.

Many bands find it restricts the type of music they are allowed to play.

This is a problem Sweet have run up against.

After a string of Wig Wam Bam type singles they found that nobody wanted them to change their bubblegum style or play the kind of music they liked.

But they rebelled — with considerable effect. Their first rock single, Blockbuster, stormed to No. 1.

"Our songs are now about 60 per cent what we want them to be, and they're getting nearer each time we release a single, drummer Mick Tucker told me.

"But don't get me wrong. I think we are, and always have been a good singles band," he said.

Having these prolific song writers Nicky Chinn and Mike Chapman to help your career in the right direction is useful too. "It's unfortunate but we have not got an ace songwriter within the band. That's not our fault, we can't all be geniuses.

"But it means we don't really command so much respect as a band like Slade who do write their own songs.

"In fact, as far as musical talent goes, were not one of the best bands, but we have a lot of other things to offer our fans.

"And I think we do a really good "live" act.

Sweet have always worked hard and done gigs all round the country. That and their chart success has led to the inevitable step — a visit to America.

"But none of us really want to go," Mick said. "We know we need to go, and financially it means a lot. But that is by far the biggest reason for going . . . as a place, it worries me.

"And I don't want to leave Pauline alone for too long . . ."

Decorating . . .

Pauline is Mick's wife — and as they were married only last year, it's not surprising that he's not keen to leave her.

They have bought a house in Ruislip, which has taken several months to decorate, and now is hardly the time Mick would want to abandon it all to disappear off to the States for months on end.

But it looks like they will be going before the year is out. Once a band have reached a certain level in this country they really have to go.

In the meantime, Sweet will not be neglecting their British fans.

Their latest album is due for release in early May. Tracks have recently been put down, and the album is something the lads have really enjoyed doing.

It includes about 70 per cent of their own material, with two or three songs from Chinn and Chapman. The title was about the last thing to cause them some concern, and it's a toss-up between Sweet F.A. and We're Revolting.

The album will fit in neatly with their latest British tour plans. They kick-off a 17-gig schedule at Bournemouth Winter Gardens on April 26 and end at Sheffield on May 24.

By that time another single may have sprung up to follow Teenage Rampage . . . but no matter how much their music changes the fans seem to love it.

And surely it cannot be long before Sweet are making records which are 100 per cent what THEY want to do. When they reach that point I've a feeling the records will still be huge hits.

● Brian Connolly . . . lead singer with Sweet, who successfully made the change from bubblegum pop to rock.

1974 / Snippets For All To Smile

Sweet cancel four dates

The Sweet, the "Teenage Rampage" hit group, have cancelled the first four dates of their British tour which was scheduled to start at Bournemouth tomorrow.

Lead singer Brian Connolly's voice broke down at rehearsals. The cancelled dates include Bournemouth, Brighton, Bristol and Plymouth.

I have looked at the 1974 diary. The band were rehearsing a lot in March/April 1974 (assuming for the UK Tour).

On 1st May David Walker advised Terry, Cuz, Bruno and myself (in the London office) that the tour was off. No reason was given.

Punch stops a pop tour

THE SWEET pop group has cancelled a seventeen-concert British tour because the lead singer Brian Connolly was injured in a gang attack.

Connolly, 25, was punched in the throat and left lying in a gutter near his home at Staines.

He was taken to hospital and it was found that his vocal chords were damaged.

The attack happened several weeks ago, but doctors say that he must continue to rest before singing again.

Damage

A little consolation for the fans who are down in the dumps over the cancellation of the Sweet's tour is the promise of a new single as soon as possible.

Lead guitarist Andy Scott says: "Hopefully, as soon as Brian's voice returns to normal, we'll make a new single to be rush-released by RCA."

Brian Connolly has been told by a specialist that if he sings within the next few weeks he could damage his larynx permanently.

Gary Glitter, who also expects to have a new single out in early July, is to make a series of concert appearances during May and June.

Dates still to be confirmed for the tour include Newcastle, Manchester, Southport and Birmingham.

Charles Fiske

Sweet date takes sour turn

CONCERT HERE

—ILLNESS

THE sweet sounds of top pop group The Sweet will not be heard in the city on Sunday May 19th after all.

A long-awaited tour by the group has been cancelled because lead singer, blond-haired Brian Connolly, is suffering from a throat condition.

Apparently Brian, who is 25, has had recurring throat trouble for the past few months and a specialist has advised him that if he sings during the next few weeks he could permanently damage his larynx.

The Sweet's lead guitarist Andy Scott says: "We are very upset about having to cancel out this tour, especially as we were scheduled to appear with The Who at the Charlton Athletic gig and it would have been a nice climax to end the tour for the fans"

"Hopefully, as soon as Brian's voice returns to normal, we will make a new single which will be rush-released to try and make up for the fans' disappointment."

As the group were due to appear at the Victoria Hall, Hanley, on May 19th, pro-

moter Mike Lloyd is asking fans to return tickets for the concert to where they bought them and money will be refunded.

He described the cancellation as "most unfortunate."

* * * *

I went back home to Shropshire and on 19th May I spoke to Andy on the phone and was told that rehearsals were cancelled so there was time off.

I didn't go back down to London until sometime in June.

ORDINATION TO BE A FAMILY AFFAIR

AN ORDINATION at St. Paul's Church, South Harrow, on June 30, will reunite three brothers, who have pursued very varied careers.

The ordinand is Mr. David Priest. His brothers are Michael Priest, who is travelling from Toronto, where he works for an oil company; and Steve Priest, guitarist with the pop group Sweet.

Their parents' home is in Grange Road, Hayes where, says the father, Mr. Norman Priest, they get people phoning all the time to ask about Steve.

June 30 will be a big day for Mrs. Margaret Priest as she is usually housebound with illness but special arrangements are being made so that she can be at the church for the ceremony.

Deacon

David was educated at Mellow Lane school and taught in the Sunday school at St. Mary's Church, Hayes. He worked in industry until he was 24 when he decided to work for the priesthood.

He then spent five years studying in theological colleges before becoming a deacon at St. Paul's a year ago.

"We are really happy at his success," said his father. "He didn't go to university so it has been a bit of a struggle for him."

The contrast between his son's careers has led to a lot of joking from Mr. Priest's friends.

"When I retired and they made a presentation my manager said: "He's got one son in oil to keep the wheels greased, one in pop so he won't be short of money and one is a priest so he's got a foot upstairs'," he said.

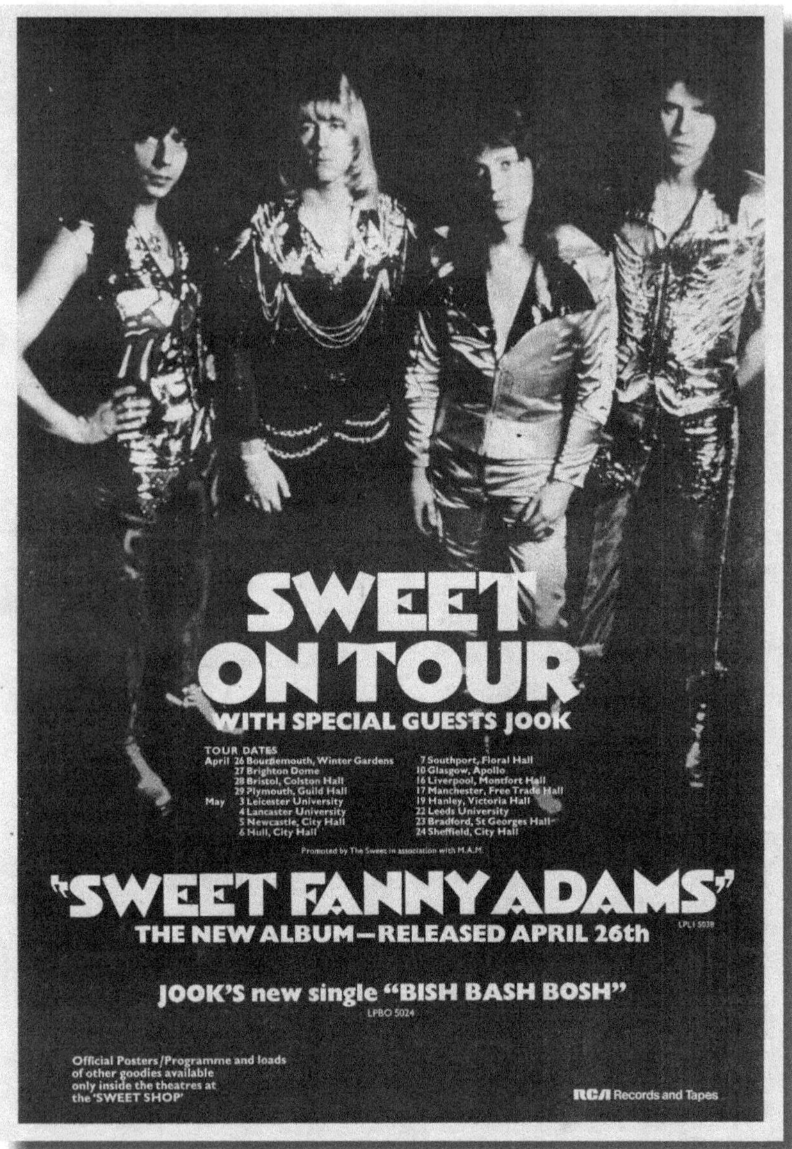
SWEET
ON TOUR
WITH SPECIAL GUESTS JOOK
TOUR DATES
April 26 Bournemouth, Winter Gardens
27 Brighton Dome
28 Bristol, Colston Hall
29 Plymouth, Guild Hall
May 3 Leicester University
4 Lancaster University
5 Newcastle, City Hall
6 Hull, City Hall
7 Southport, Floral Hall
10 Glasgow, Apollo
16 Liverpool, Montfort Hall
17 Manchester, Free Trade Hall
19 Hanley, Victoria Hall
22 Leeds University
23 Bradford, St Georges Hall
24 Sheffield, City Hall
Promoted by The Sweet in association with M.A.M.
"SWEET FANNY ADAMS"
THE NEW ALBUM—RELEASED APRIL 26th
LPL1 5038
JOOK'S new single "BISH BASH BOSH"
LPBO 5024
Official Posters/Programme and loads
of other goodies available
only inside the theatres at
the 'SWEET SHOP'
RCA Records and Tapes

Thursday 4th July: I went to a party hosted by Steve with Bruno and Cuz for a US Independence Day do. Very nice, very enjoyable, hosted well, and of course as usual Steve was the nicest, affable guy you could be with. I never heard Steve boast about himself or the band particularly, he just tended to go along with it all, unless there was something specific he wasn't happy with, but that doesn't mean he didn't give it his "all".

One of three Priests lives up to his name

David Priest has a name he lived up to on Saturday when he was ordained in St. Paul's Cathedral.

And his two brothers who have been successful in completely contrasting careers — without reference to their surname — were there to watch.

David Priest has been deacon at St. Paul's Church, South Harrow, for the past year. His brother, Michael (left above, pouring a celebration drink) flew from Toronto, Canada, where he works for an oil company, and his other brother is known to many youngsters as he is Steve Priest, guitarist with the successful Sweet pop group.

The family live in Hayes where their mother, Mrs. Margaret Priest, is normally housebound. Special arrangements were made to transport her to the cathedral for the ordination service.

Monday 8th July: All went to Granada TV and the guys performed on the show *Lift Off.* A good show.

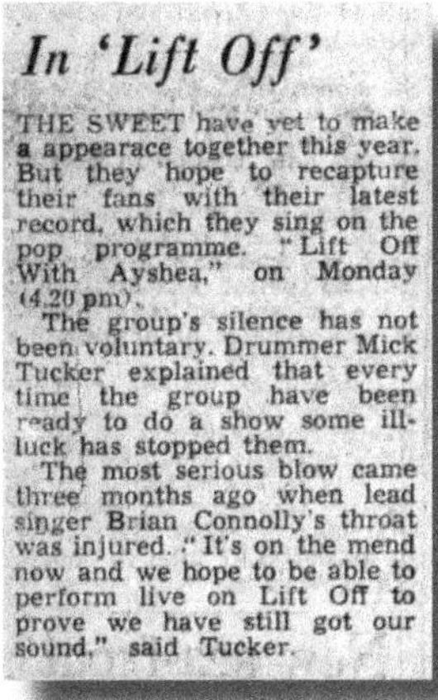

In 'Lift Off'

THE SWEET have yet to make a appearace together this year. But they hope to recapture their fans with their latest record, which they sing on the pop programme. "Lift Off With Ayshea," on Monday (4.20 pm).

The group's silence has not been voluntary. Drummer Mick Tucker explained that every time the group have been ready to do a show some ill-luck has stopped them.

The most serious blow came three months ago when lead singer Brian Connolly's throat was injured. "It's on the mend now and we hope to be able to perform live on Lift Off to prove we have still got our sound," said Tucker.

Monday 15th July: Andy, Jackie and their son Damien came to my house and we took them for a spin down the River Thames in my boat, to Penton Hook Lock near Staines and back, they came into my house afterwards and we all had a nice chat.

Friday 19th July: Now this is great... Brian came to meet me and we both went down the River Thames on his boat to a Marina because he wanted to tell them that his boat was lacking in performance. At this point Andy arrived to put a deposit on a boat for himself, a Sea Master 813. That same evening the crew and band all went to London for a photo shoot. Andy and Brian wore sailor's caps... (Just kidding).

Tuesday 23rd July: Before going to a rehearsal in Hillingdon in Middlesex Brian had seen another boat he wanted to buy and he and I both went to have a look at it, after which we headed back to the rehearsal.

After the rehearsal Brian wanted to show Mick Angus our tour manager the boat he was buying. We all went to look, then back to Brian's for a Spaghetti Bolognese... Yummy.

Saturday 27th July: I went and met Terry and Cuz from the road crew as we had some errands to run for the band. I had run out of "float" (a term for useable cash in those days) So Terry had £5 ready for me, 5 pounds! Can you imagine £5 now? Two cups of tea if you are lucky.

Monday 29th July: This was a big day for me really. The crew and I were at Hemel Hempstead Pavilion as we were meeting the guys who had just completed building a new sound system and a fabulous new mixing desk for the band. I was over the moon as you might expect with this fabulous new custom-built mixing desk. It was a beauty.

Tuesday 30th July: Crew and band all at the Pavilion to test the new system. Oh my God it was beautiful and made a great band even better. I was in seventh heaven.

Thursday 8th August: Now this little piece is amazing. It shows where the band were in the public's eyes. I was on Brian's boat with him and Phillip, his neighbour, heading out to that great big ocean, the English Channel. We stopped at Shell Haven to top up with fuel (top up! It was 75 gallons) the guy selling the fuel recognised Brian and said that's just £5 to you and Brian gave him a signed record. P.S The night before we ran out of fuel and had been towed to the fuel station by a Police boat (I wasn't going to tell you that.)

Thursday 12th September: The band and crew were all at Audio International recording studios. Recordings were being made all day. It was a long day.

I went out as the recording was coming to an end and bought some booze to take back to the studio. I got well drunk and crashed out on the sofa in the studio. This is the good bit; I was taken home in the limousine with the other band members except Brian. He drove my minivan home for me. What a cool guy eh?

****

Sad beyond words — this was hard to write: We had a gig lined up for Wednesday 2nd October in Helsinki in Finland. None of us musically or otherwise had been to Finland, so there was an extra bit of anticipation there to see something different. The world was much bigger then than it is now.

It started on the 1st October with the crew and I leaving Gothenburg at about 7:00am and Cuz driving to Stockholm. We boarded the boat to Finland and passed through the Stockholm Archipelago and climbed into bed at 11:55 pm.

We woke up at 7:40 am, had breakfast and watched our arrival into Helsinki. Everything was searched by Customs (personal stuff), they then took us by car to our hotel, called the Hotel Kantero. We had a meal and then went to our rooms for a sleep and rest.

Terry later woke me with the awful news that something had happened to my three and half year-old daughter, Victoria (God knows what?) and that David Walker had called Terry from England and had booked me a flight back to England and to get me to Helsinki airport as soon as possible.

I thought God may she please be okay. I was getting packed, when Terry came back to my room and said to me, and I shall never forget these exact words, "I don't know how to tell you this, but your daughter died this morning."

Terry and Cuz took me to Helsinki airport, where amazingly the band were just coming through arrivals and dear Brian came walking over to me. He said, "Is it true about Victoria", I said "Yes I'm on the next flight back to England" he said to me, (get this one) "Jan, would you like me to come back to England with you?" Now that is an absolutely wonderful person.

I hugged him, and I said something along the lines of, "Brian as much I would love you to be with me for this dreadful trip home, you have a very important bunch of concerts you have to do, but I will never, never forget you offering to come with me".

WHAT A GUY!

I was in a trance for most of that trip and was met by Rod, the band's chauffeur at Heathrow airport.

It was then a three-and-a-half-hour drive back to Newport in Shropshire, my home at that time. He was just marvellous with me/ for me, for that whole journey. Upon arrival I said come and have a coffee before you return. He said, "No, now is your time. I will head straight back."

I went into my house and my wife Pat was there with my son Paul, who was five years old, and my parents. I can't even try to explain the feeling going through everyone (I even heard Victoria moving about in her bedroom, although she was of course at the mortuary).

The following morning a wonderful Policeman friend took us to the mortuary. Oh my God, she had died suddenly of Acute Laryngotracheobronchitis causing asphyxia, the closing up of the windpipe. Why, why, why? The funeral was on Tuesday 8th October.

The following Tuesday I was back on a plane heading for the German part of the tour, a very difficult decision but my wife was very strong and said, "life must go on." She was right, life must go on.

On Tuesday 15th October I met Andy and management and the slightly changed road crew, and we boarded a plane for Germany and a gig at the Musikhalle. The last gig of the tour was on Monday 28th October. I felt pretty flat for the rest of 1974.

Rock band cancel again

by JAMES BELSEY

Top rock band Sweet have cancelled their concert at Bristol's Colston Hall tonight.

Refunds are being made at the hall's box office, and staff will be kept on tonight to give refunds to ticket-holders who have not heard of the cancellation.

Mr. Norman Divall, a spokesman for publicists Tony Barrow International who handle the band, said: "The band have had no alternative but to pull out of the Bristol concert.

"The promotors of the concert have breached their contract and the band cannot play."

The cancellation follows two others on the group's current British tour. Earlier two shows were cancelled because lead guitarist Andy Scott went down with stomach troubles.

And it is the second time this year that Sweet have failed to appear for scheduled concerts at the Colston Hall.

Their spring show was cancelled when lead singer Brian Connolly lost his voice.

Tonight's performance was to have been a replacement for that gig.

Some 500 tickets had been sold for tonight's concert in the 2,000-seater hall.

Now it's sweet and sour

FEW groups are the subject of more diverse opinions these days than Sweet: sweet and sour is dish of the day when the critics discuss their professed progression to something more meaningful than their early kiddi-rock songles.

Chapman and Chinn singles make money but not, apparently, reputations, so "Desolation Boulevard" is announced as yet another bid to get Brian Connolly and Co., recognised as "a fully fledged group" whatever that may be.

For the sour brigade, Sweet will never make it — they just are not good enough. For those of a sweeter disposition they are coming on well, steadily overcoming their limitations. Put me down with the latter group; to be honest I cannot see what the fuss is about.

Spin this album without looking back or forward and it is an entertaining assortment of pop and rock and mid-heavy material. Some to dance to, some to listen to — a few to exercise your mind, a few to exercise your feet. Connolly's voice is losing its teenybopper twang and drummer Mick Tucker is no longer simply pounding out the basic beat. (RCA).

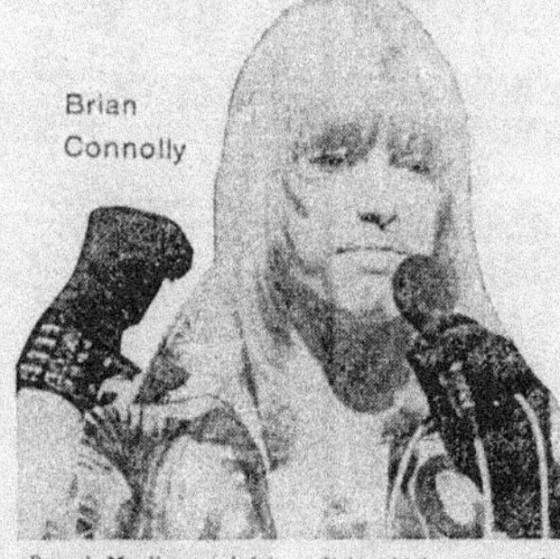

Brian Connolly

Russel Mael's weird falsetto guaranteed Sparks a degree of individuality when they first hit the pop scene. It was a gimmick which could so quickly have faded, but imaginative writing by Russel and his brother Ron has maintained the band's magnetic orginality.

"Propaganda" is in the same crazy vein as their early single hits and whether or not you like their nerve jangling style you have got to admire their ability to sound so different from everyone else.

It is a high power performance from the off with every track a winner as the boys rock, bounce and swing through 11 numbers. Witty, weird and wonderful (Island).

Jolly

"C'Est La Vie" — McGuinness Flint: A strong country rocker with Lou Stonebridge blowing and sucking in fine style on his harmonica sets this commendable latest from Mc F on its way. There is a jolly country romp sound to the whole album, with the odd ballad fitting perfectly into the format as a pleasant chance to catch your breath. I rate this album as good as any recent offering from the boys (Bronze).

"The Rock 'n' Soul Story" — Vocal groups (Platters, Diamonds), instrumental groups (Champs), white rock bands (Freddy Bell) and black r and b bands doing their 50's and 60's hits on a bargain price double album. Great to hear the half-dozen real classics again, but the rest sound a little dated with their wailing saxes and silly chorus lines (Philips).

Relaxed

"Highway Call" — Richard Betts: Quiet man of the great Allman Bros. Band, Betts steps forward for a solo album spot. Lots of good support from his friends down in Georgia results in six pleasant, relaxed examples of southern country rock on side one. Side two features Betts and his guitar in just two numbers which might almost be classed as jazz (Capricorn).

"Christmas Album" — Frank Sinatra: Seasonal fare from one of the all time greats. All the expected songs, including "Jingle Bells," "Have Yourself A Merry Little Christmas" and Mel Torme's "Christmas Song" and six carols. The whole album is superbly sung

When things weren't so sweet for pop star

TWO things please Brian Connolly, lead singer of Sweet, about the Top Ten success of "Fox On The Run."

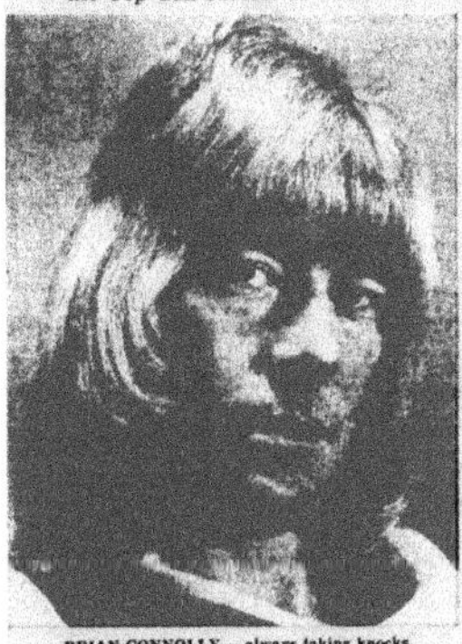

BRIAN CONNOLLY — always taking knocks.

a cop but as a singer.

"I sing with a jazz band most weekends and I would like to make a record," he said.

"But it would have to be an offshoot of my acting career. I wouldn't like to become a pop star. They're just puppets."

One: It is the first A-side single penned and produced by the band and not by their former Svengali duo, Nicky Chinn and Mike Chapman, writes **Alan Goddard**.

Two: It is the first single on which the blonde-haired singer reckons he has performed with his former power following an unprovoked street gang attack a year ago.

Connolly was savagely beaten up and kicked 10 times in the throat near his home at Staines, Surrey. His vocal chords were so badly damaged that it looked as if his career was wrecked.

"That was a knock and a half," he said. "The specialist said it was going to take a year for my voice to come back. And he was right.

No power

"My voice gradually improved over the months right up to this record. You've only to listen to that and compare it with anything else I've done in the last 12 months — before there was no power, clarity or range.

"It was frightening when it happened. I could not talk at all, just whisper. I was double worried."

Connolly, 26, has been a musician for 12 years — and has the scars to prove it. In the last mugging, he had 18 stitches inserted in his head and 17 in the mouth.

In the past, he has been attacked by a gang of "leather boys" after an engagement, knifed in the stomach and a boisterous fan, trying to cut his hair, dug the scissors in his scalp.

"I'm always taking knocks," shrugged Connolly. "I fell down the stairs four weeks ago and broke my ankle."

Was pop idol-bashing an occupational hazard?

"Well, a few things I could have avoided," he answered. "It's just that I've got a bad temper. I hate to walk away from a scrap just because people think: 'Oh, he's a pop star'.

"A lot of these blokes don't reckon you're a human being. They think they can give you any old rap

"But occasionally work gets right on top of you. You reach the point where you don't want to take it any more. So you just retaliate."

Eight years

The consistent Sweet, who celebrate eight years of musical togetherness next month, have taken and survived critical blows. But now they're doing it their way.

Connolly explained the go-it-alone policy as a mutual agreement between Sweet and Chinn and Chapman, who strung together 10 successive hits for the group.

"They've learned from us and anything we've learned from them has now come to a full stop," he said. "But, if they come up with a song, we'll do it.

"At least now we'll get the respect that we are not being led on a collar by other people. The attitude used to be that we made good singles, but the backbone was Chinn and Chapman.

"Now there's no more of that. Really, this is like a beginning for us because we're going to produce everything that is ours and not other people's."

1975

Thursday 9th January: My wife and I had Andy and his wife Jackie round to our house for drinks and then on to a nice Indian restaurant. These were good times to talk uninterrupted with ideas for the band.

Friday 7th February: This is unusual — we took Sweet's sound system to the Rainbow Theatre in London, to give a demo to Argent, another great band at the time.

Tuesday 25th March: I went to Andy's house to listen to the A.D.T. effect (automatic double-tracking) that Andy had got from Revox. Interesting. Lots of rehearsals and equipment upgrades over this period.

April: A big tour of Scandinavia from early April and into the start of May in Germany.

Monday 12th May: Kingsway Recorders, London. Andy and Mike were there with a keyboard player, Fiachra Trench, to add a piano and Elka string machine to 'Lady Starlight'. Turned out really awesome. This has always been my favourite track.

Although this track was released on *Desolation Boulevard* in November 1974. I checked my diary, so this must have been a re-recording or they just decided to add some overdubs.

Take a listen and watch this being performed on YouTube by Andy and Sweet in 1991 at the Capitol Theatre in Hanover, Germany. Beautifully done, beautifully recorded and I have spoken to a guy from the sound company who recorded it and he said nothing was remixed before it went on YouTube. It is superb.

EUROPEAN ROCK MUSIC POLLS
POP MAGAZINE POLL 1975

Top Group
1. SWEET
2. Deep Purple
3. ELP
4. Yes
5. Pink Floyd

Top Singer
1. BRIAN CONNOLLY
2. Robert Plant
3. Ian Gillan
4. Jon Anderson
5. Peter Gabriel

Top Bassist
1. Glenn Hughes
2. STEVE PRIEST
3. Greg Lake
4. Jack Bruce
5. Chris Squire

Top Drummer
1. Carl Palmer
2. Ian Paice
3. MICK TUCKER
4. Keith Moon
5. Nick Mason

Top Guitarist
1. Ritchie Blackmore
2. Eric Clapton
3. Rory Gallagher
4. ANDY SCOTT
5. Jimi Hendrix

MUSIEK EXPRESS POLL 1975

Top Recording Group
1. SWEET
2. Yes
3. ELP
4. Deep Purple

Top Vocalist
1. David Bowie
2. BRIAN CONNOLLY
3. Jon Anderson
4. Ian Gillan

Top Live Group
1. ELP
2. SWEET
3. Yes
4. Deep Purple
5. Genesis

Top Drummer
1. Carl Palmer
2. Pete York
3. Ian Paice
4. MICK TUCKER
5. Ginger Baker

FIRST PLACE WINNERS (FOR THREE YEARS IN A ROW) BRAVO MAGAZINE POLL 1975

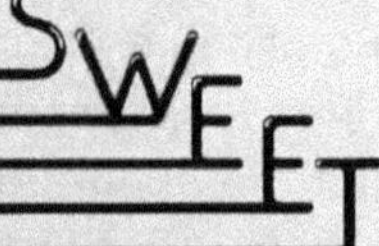

The Album
DESOLATION BOULEVARD
ST-11395

Includes The Single
BALLROOM BLITZ
(4055)

SWEET HAS SOLD 26 MILLION RECORDS AND RECEIVED 28 GOLD AND SILVER
DISC AWARDS AROUND THE WORLD...AND THEIR NEW ALBUM IN
AMERICA IS ON CAPITOL RECORDS AND TAPES.

SWEET

Capitol

Acclaimed the newest force in rock music
after an incredible "live" performance at their Sold Out
concert appearance in Los Angeles, Europe's top-selling band
has broken through with their Top 10 single,
Ballroom Blitz,
from their hit album,
Desolation Boulevard, (ST-11395)
which includes their newest single,

Fox On The Run. (4157)

Soon On National Tour

Friday 1st August: I am putting this info in, for you to imagine this journey in 1975. All went to Heathrow Airport London, boarded Air New Zealand DC10. Flight Number BA599 departed at 4:30pm. Arrived in Los Angeles at 4:00am in the morning UK time, went through immigration at 8:30pm LA time. Boarded the same plane again. Took off at 10:30 pm LA time. Arrived in Tahiti approximately 3:00am to refuel. Took off and flew for another 11 hours approximately and arrived in Auckland at 7:30am New Zealand time. As you can imagine we were all like Zombies by this time. There was time for sleep though, because the first gig wasn't until the 9th August because of all the sound equipment arriving.

Sunday 10th August: Founders Theatre, Hamilton. A band called Beech supporting us as it did the night before in Auckland.

Wednesday 13th August: Town Hall, Wellington. A great gig with support band Tapestry. (They were really good too).

Thursday 14th August: Wellington to Christchurch flight. Boeing 737 flight. Day Off. Trevor Griffin (one of the road crew) and I rented a *Holden* car and drove to Arthur's Pass National Park. Hairy road but all very beautiful.

POP SCENE

It's Sweet on the run

By PHIL SCOTT

WHILE Steeleye Span were receiving plenty of publicity this week The Sweet slipped into town with scarcely a whisper.

And that seems a little unusual for a group which has sold a staggering 15 million records and has Fox On The Run sitting at the top of the Australian charts.

In recent years The Sweet have churned out top 10 material so consistently that critics dubbed them a "hit factory."

Mick Tucker, the group's drummer, this week dismissed the phenomenal success of their singles in a sentence.

"We could write 10 hits like Fox On The Run in a week but that's not what we're aiming for," he said.

"We want to capture in four minutes what our music is all about, and at the same time display the individual talents we have."

Not a bad statement coming from a group who were told by the songwriting experts that their compositions were hopeless.

When the group formed back in 1967 they achieved moderate success and it wasn't until they met their managers Mike Chapman and Nicky Chinn that their ascent to pop stardom began.

Chapman and Chinn wrote many of the group's songs but split with The Sweet in "unfortunate circumstances" last year.

"We were brainwashed into thinking that we couldn't write our own songs," Mick Tucker recalled.

"We've progressed a lot since then."

The Sweet have a reputation for being an electric stage act, very physical and with optical effects designed to pack a powerful wallop.

Their stage act has been refined to the most minute detail — back projection, freeze framing during a drum battle sequence, eye-catching lighting and an exacting sound set up must all work perfectly.

If they don't The Sweet have been known to vent their frustration on their very expensive instruments — more than one guitar has been smashed to pieces after a technical mishap held up the show.

"We've been accused of being childish, but when we've put so much into rehearsing the act and some mechanical hitch spoils it, I think we're entitled to be angry," Mick Tucker said.

On-stage The Sweet are outlandishly clad, instrument-smashing rock idols.

Off-stage they look "straight," right down to their immaculately groomed hair.

The impression they convey is one of "scrubbed behind the ears" freshness — hardly what one expects from a multi-million selling rock group.

The group's only Sydney concert is on August 18 at the Hordern Pavilion.

Friday 15th August 1975: Town Hall, Christchurch. The support band Freshwater were a good band too. Ugh! Ouch... As Sweet were coming on for their set, Andy fell off the stage. There was a short delay, he was a bit dazed and had a grazed leg. Thank God it wasn't worse... Imagine having to cancel a tour this far away from home.

Saturday 16th August: I drove to Regent Theatre, Dunedin — myself in a Toyota van full of lighting equipment for the gig. This was an excellent gig (New Zealanders are very charming people, it makes a big difference).

Sunday 17th August: We drove to Dunedin airport. All got the flight to Christchurch. Meal and rested a while. Later got continuing flight on a *Qantas* Jumbo at 3:50pm for the flight to Sydney, Australia. Arrived two hours, fifty minutes later (but two hours earlier because of the time difference). Their status was growing rapidly and Sweet were pretty much a worldwide band.

Every country had its own feeling and pros and cons. I don't think anyone had a particular favourite as every country had its own merits. When we arrived at Sydney airport, it must have been a bit like what the Beatles felt, it was absolutely full of fans, including the roof of the main terminal. It was incredibly inspiring for all to see after all the hard work. All crashed out at the Town House Hotel.

Monday 18th August: After nearly twelve hours sleep and after breakfast, we, the crew all went to the airport to load all of the equipment into a *Jand's* hire truck and set off to the gig at the Hordern Pavilion. Got set up and the band did their sound check. Ed Leffler the band's American manager had flown over. The band was supported by Andy Gibb brother of Barry, Robin and Maurice Gibb of the Bee Gees. This wasn't the best gig in the world as I think everyone was totally exhausted.

Tuesday 19th August: The next night's gig was Melbourne. A good gig, wonderful audience, but the acoustics of the Festival Hall were not good.

Friday 22nd August: Entertainment Centre, Perth. At the end of this concert, we got a 2:00am flight to Adelaide for the gig at the Apollo Stadium on the 23rd. This Australian tour finished at Festival Hall, Brisbane on Saturday 30th August.

Sunday 31st August: We took a flight from Brisbane to Sydney for the long haul to Los Angeles. The Pan Am jumbo at Brisbane had a fuel leak and we had a four-hour delay. (A fuel leak!) Arrived in L.A that evening and checked in to the Holiday Inn in Hollywood. Got to bed at 3:50am.

Monday 1st September: All went well in the car up the Pacific Coast Highway to Zuma beach beyond Malibu. A good time was being had by all, laying on the beach in the afternoon, having a Mexican meal in the early evening and then on for a drink at a 'British Pub' followed by a visit to the Great American Food and Beverage Company. The barman and the barmaids sang and played guitars and piano etc. A bit different to a night out in London.

Wednesday 3rd September: Meal at the Chart House restaurant on Redondo Beach. Magnificent meal. The next days were to relax just enjoying ourselves. We visited Capitol Records and listened to albums, went to the beach at Santa Monica for a few hours and sunbathed and swam. Enjoyed ourselves at the cinema and did some shopping, ate good pizzas, went to Disney Land. My wife had joined me at this point and we spent the next few days exploring the area.

There were two more gigs in September:

Thursday 11th September: Paramount Theatre, Seattle.

Saturday 13th September: Civic Auditorium, Santa Monica.

Monday 15th September: I went to downtown L.A for a look around, car broke down. My friend and I had a look under the bonnet and a car crashed into us from behind. Carrie, my friend was hurt. Police and ambulance arrived. I went with the breakdown truck and Carrie went to hospital. She had an X-ray and had a fractured shoulder. We were then sent to another hospital, dreadful place, sat for four hours before she was seen.

The following day I got a flight to Vancouver and was met by my Uncle and Auntie and got the ferry across to Galiano Island to relax until the 19th before flying back to England.

Friday 3rd October: Took a lot of Andy's gear around to his house for him to be able to write music and check out new sounds etc.

Tuesday 7th October: I don't really remember this but we supplied Black Sabbath with the PA equipment for a while.

Sunday 12th October: Sweet's PA hired for The Drifters at Hammersmith Odeon which we set up for them. They were incredibly amazing.

Friday 17th October 1975: Totally irrelevant but I passed my motorcycle test.

Tuesday 21st / Wednesday 22nd October 1975: Band at Kingsway Recorders. Sorry but I don't have the details in my diary of what they mixed.

Friday 28th November 1975: Band and Crew at De Lane Lea Studios to record 'Lady Starlight' for *Supersonic* television show. Went well.

December 1975: Time off for everyone, time spent with families. Yeah — normality break.

For The Sweet – how sweet it is

By CAMERON CROWE
Rolling Stone

MUNICH — Here in Germany, as well as the rest of the continent, Brian Connolly, Steve Priest, Mick Tucker and Andy Scott — The Sweet — are demigods.

Their concerts are synonymous with riots and their five-year-long string of European hits has yet to be broken. No other group has threatened The Sweet stronghold. Not even the Bay City Rollers.

"Those Rollers," snickers Brian Connolly during a break from the band's sessions at Munich's Musicland Studios. "Just look at them with their funny clothes and nervous determination to become the biggest band in the world."

His thoughts crystallized with help from the syrup-like German beer. "The Sweet just don't care. Everyone tells us we have to scheme on an American audience, if we really want to hit it big. Ha! When we get there, we'll play what we want to play. And if we don't go over well, we'll do concerts here. This is a rock and roll band, not an army."

Already, The Sweet has fared better with an American following than such overseas favorites as Suzi Quatro, Gary Glitter, Alvin Stardust or the Sensational Alex Harvey Band. Perhaps significantly, its recent Top Five U. S. hit, "Ballroom Blitz," was not exploited with a garish publicity campaign. This band is above that.

"We're-huge-in-Europe-now-it's-your-turn type," says bassist Steve Priest. "I'm not surprised those other groups failed. They're average bands. Not outstanding at all. Look at Slade. They're just an English football band that had a few hits, aren't they? On the other hand, we're not just some artificial singles band."

It's taken The Sweet seven years to make that claim.

When the group was first formed in 1969 by Connolly and drummer Mick Tucker (both of Wainwright's Gentlemen, the band that later gave Ian Gillan and Roger Glover to Deep Purple), its main objective was hit singles. After the first four attempts failed to shake up the charts, a meeting was arranged with Britain's Bacharach and David of punk-rock — Nicky Chinn and Mike Chapman.

The result, "Funny Funny," was The Sweet's first smash.

Some 12 more Chinn and Chapman-penned hits followed, racking up a worldwide sales mark of 20 million units. The only four singles released in the United States ('Little Willy,' 'Blockbuster,' 'Wig-Wam Bam,' and 'Hell Raiser') sold well, but a quickly assembled compilation album on Bell Records didn't.

Purposely, they say, the band ignored offers for an American tour.

The Sweet — Steve Priest, Brian Connolly, Mick Tucker and Andy Scott.

"We thought that the only reason 'Little Willy' was a hit in the States was because people thought it was a black record," remembers Connolly. "Besides, at the time we were wearing makeup and dressing up like four Christmas trees. It was a giggle for us.

"People like Bowie were taking it really seriously, and we were just a bunch of tarts having a good time. If we'd gone to the States two years ago, when the glitter rat race was on, we would have been misunderstood. It would have killed us. We did the right thing by staying away. No question."

The turning point came in early 1974 when, in the course of a London pub brawl, Connolly's throat was kicked in. In the months he (and the group) was out of commission, The Sweet reassessed its direction. "We had been getting Number Ones just like that," Steve Priest says and snaps his fingers nonchalantly. "We were on top of it all. But we weren't getting off at all. All those early hits . . . they were crap."

The Sweet informed Chinn and Chapman that their services would no longer be needed. The first totally band-written and produced single, "Fox on the Run" — just released in the States — was a major European success earlier this year.

"There's no bad feelings between Nicky and Mike and us," says guitarist Andy Scott. "I don't think they're capable of writing the right kind of material for us anymore. I mean, they can pick up unknown groups and come up with the commercial goods, but what we're talking about is our own music."

The Sweet's American following, however, is still on time delay, due to a switch in labels. It left Bell when its contract expired in June, and recently released the first Capitol album, "Desolation Boulevard." It's another compilation record 5 of the 10 tracks are Chinn-Chapman compositions.

"Capitol picked the songs for the album," admits Priest. "If we'd had our say, we'd have had all our own tracks on it, obviously. Which is not to say it's a bum album. We didn't do too badly, considering some of the ludicrous stuff they wanted to put in there . . . we had a real fight on our hands. We're way beyond most of that stuff now. 'Ballroom Blitz' is two years old, for example. Let's not forget that. We wouldn't have put that out."

After playing one experimental gig at the sold-out Santa Monica Civic Auditorium, The Sweet has gone ahead and booked an extensive American tour to begin in January. Coinciding with the tour will be the worldwide release of a new, current Sweet album.

"We're trying not to compromise on this one; this is the step we've always wanted to take," proclaims drummer Mick Tucker, "and if we don't make it, I guess that's it. Just another 15-hit wonder."

At London Airport, June 1975.

November 23, 1974
SOUNDS   Page 29
FILTHY
HONDA
BACK BY POPULAR
DEMAND
BROHTER JOHN
DESOLATION BOULEVARD
SWEET·THE ALBUM LPL1 5080
SWEET DATES   NOV 21 Sunderland Locarno
30 Leicester University
DEC 3 Salford University
5 Middlesbrough Town Hall
6 Hull University
7 Imperial College, London
10 Colston Hall, Bristol
11 Town Hall, Birmingham
RCA
ALSO AVAILABLE ON TAPE

At Skansen
Amusement Park,
Stockholm, April 1975.

Change Of Tack

Brian was a very good, nice guy. They all were. When he was in my band we had some good times together. He was a little under confident believe it or not, but that was Brian.

Everyone he met immediately took to him. He always had a good story to tell and enjoyed life to the full. We used to do things together and always enjoyed each other's company. When he bought his boat (*'Francis Lee'*) he used to keep it moored at my father's house, a waterfront house on the River Thames, just along from Staines in Middlesex.

We used to spend downtime going for a little cruise down to Hampton Court or towards Oxford. All very peaceful and relaxing. Brian was a guy that needed to de-stress.

The trip down through London was mentioned earlier. We talked about that for years, especially heading out into the English Channel and doing some real boating.

As the years went on and the success was growing at an enormous rate, I would see that Brian was struggling a bit with the glory of it all, but I don't believe the fans tuned into this, they just loved him more and more.

The pressure of the job and having to be on public display along with very little down time, I am sure created a lot of problems for someone prone to anxiety, as Brian was.

He was one of the best front men out there doing his stuff and that was getting everyone excited, ecstatic, enjoying all the band, buying their singles and albums and going to as many Sweet concerts as they could... Worldwide.

Once we were travelling all over the globe I didn't get as much time to see Brian socially, which was a great shame.

Brian always enjoyed his drink (which was common knowledge) and I feel sure that the management and band members would have done their best to help him. Like many successful artists, becoming famous is not necessarily the 'best medicine' for cruising through life without a care. The more sensitive amongst us can, and do, look for support in other ways.

The last time I saw Brian perform on stage was in the mid-1990s in Oxford, England. I went backstage during the interval, and he was so very pleased to see me.

Towards the end he became a bit of a recluse and several times I tried to make contact but to no avail. The rest is sadly history. RIP Brian.

****

I first met Andy, as mentioned near the beginning of this book, when all the guys came back to my house in Newport, Shropshire, after doing a gig nearby. My wife Patricia was there also and we all got into a very interesting conversation. I was telling them what I had done the last few years and they reciprocated (how lives can change so quickly). Well towards the end of all the chat and coffees etc, I am not sure which one it was that said this, I believe it may have been Andy, who said... We need a new sound engineer for live gigs, would you be interested?

It must have taken (including getting a nod from my wife) at least, hmmm, yes at least five seconds to say I would love to. I had very rapidly put into my mind that there would be a lot of time away, but also a lot of time at home, albeit working our butts off. But that was fine, I already, from the concert that evening, knew that they were going to be huge and wanted to help push that along with my love of music and giving the guys the sound they wanted. So yes my life changed a great deal after saying yes that evening. Thank you all you guys up there and Andy down here...

****

Steve. Well... If you can imagine, a very calm and collected guy with not a bad word to say about anyone or anything, unless it was really necessary to speak up, which he did with great tact (usually). Steve was so laid back most of the time and nothing seemed to bother him particularly. I don't even remember him raising his voice.

I believe it was good that there was 'a Steve' in the band because he was often the one that intervened in situations that needed calming down.

He had an amazing, but subtle sense of humour, many times he sounded almost serious when in fact he was taking the piss.

You could tell Steve was thinking, just from his demeanour. He was very blessed to meet Maureen, his future wife, as she was very respectful of him and a very kind, lovely person. Of course she was with him for all those years through to his very sad premature death. RIP Steve.

****

Mick Tucker. What a drummer! One of the best out there.

Mick's trump card was his passion and perfection behind a drum kit. He was in my band along with Brian for a while and I was always in awe watching and listening to him in his constant rhythms and fill-ins and his wont to be the best out there. His passion was endless and he was the eternal perfectionist.

He just got better and better and once in Sweet he zoomed to new heights in his feel, technique and most of all in Sweet with his double screen drum solo answering himself along with the screen sound behind. It was unbelievable, probably one of the most talked about things with Sweet fans. They went crazy at concerts. It made us all feel so good to be involved with this level of talent.

Can you imagine not having YouTube where we can watch the guys in concert whenever we want?

Mick Angus, Tour Manager
Well here was a really nice guy who did a great job looking after the band whilst touring. I can't remember how long he was with the band but he was usually calm and collected and worth his weight in gold. The band sometimes gave him a hard time, i.e. if anything wasn't going according to plan, (meaning everything like the hotel

not good, food at gig not good, Anything, it was "Mick sort this out!") Having said that there was a great deal of respect amongst everyone, just that sometimes a verbal explosion helps, but apologies were always forthcoming.

Entec Lighting / projection team
Pat Chapman, Pete Challenger, Martin Nicholas and Fiona and a whole bunch of others over the years. Now this was a really professional bunch of people. They knew their job down to the last detail and just got on and did it.

Pete Challenger had the job of screen projection on to the huge screens, one on each side of, and behind Mick and his enormous drum kit, which included tympani drums and anything else you could imagine. Just this alone was a spectacle to excite the eyes and brain as the gig was creating an atmosphere that is too hard to imagine, unless you were actually there.

Sweet were a world leading band — make no mistake...

1976

Now if I can remember correctly this was an excellent year. Let's head into my diary…

Sunday 18th January: Off we go again! Went to Heathrow airport, rest of the crew plus the band there... Long journey ahead. Flight from Heathrow to Washington DC with Pan Am. Changed to a Delta flight to Atlanta, then another to Chattanooga. Phew, all checked in to the Hilton Hotel.

Tuesday 20th January: Soundcheck all day.

Wednesday 21st January: Gig at Chattanooga Memorial Auditorium.
Had breakfast then went to the gig and sound checked until 2:00pm. The Eric Carmen Band arrived and set up and did their soundcheck. First concert of the tour and all went well. This was the beginning of a very long tour.

I am going to list all of the gigs and dates but only write comments about anything special (It was all special but you know what I mean).

22nd January: Nashville, Tennessee, War Memorial Auditorium. Eric Carmen was going to be the support act for the entire tour.

23rd January: Terra Haute, Hulman Civic Centre, University Centre.

24th January: Travelling (you are going to love this). Got to Columbus Ohio at 7:30pm after 275 miles drive and checked in to the Holiday Inn. Crew all went to Seafood Bay restaurant. I had

SWEET
"GIVE US A WINK!"
The latest album by Europe's
most acclaimed new band! Includes
"Action."
Capitol
NOW ON NATIONAL TOUR!

a mixed seafood dish plus a coffee and cherry liqueur brandy, a Drambuie and half a bottle of wine. Then we went to a club where I had four Screwdrivers. I got a bit lightheaded. Believe me, not every night was like this.

25th, 26th and 27th January: We were off. Just as well.

28th January: Veteran Memorial Auditorium, Columbus Ohio. Three bands tonight (including Styx, a great band).

29th January: Convention Centre, Indianapolis, Indiana.

30th January: Aragon Ballroom, Chicago. Three bands here, Artful Dodger, Eric Carmen and Sweet. It was wonderful as you can imagine to be headlining the concerts.

31st January: Music Hall, Cleveland Ohio.

1st February: Civic Centre, Charleston, West Virginia. Good gig but I started feeling quite ill at the end of the show. Sore throat, shooting pains etc (exhaustion?)

2nd February: Woke up feeling awful, Chronic headache and aches and pains. I was taken to hospital with another of our crew members (Flo- Florence), real name Lawrence, Ha Ha.

We were in hospital for four hours and were given a penicillin jab and a prescription for Ampicillin capsules plus vitamin C capsules. (cause- Upper respiratory infection) Last thing we needed on a major tour.

3rd February: Laid in, feeling rough.

4th February: Still feeling lousy. Thank goodness this happened on days with no concerts. Although we travelled all through this night on way to Lewiston, Maine for the next gig.

5th February: We played Lewiston, Maine. At the end of the gig we departed for Boston at 3:00am. Got stopped by the police for no back lights. Spent two hours in the services having them fixed. Got to Boston hotel at 9:00am. Slept until 10:30am and then went to gig and set up all over again.

After this gig we set off for Buffalo, New York and arrived at 1:00pm (484 miles). This was an incredibly long, hard but very successful tour. These concerts followed on from Buffalo:

8th February: Toronto.

12th February: Pittsburgh.

13th February: Philadelphia.

14th February: Kutztown.

15th February: Richmond.

18th February: Memphis.

20th February: Jacksonville.

21st February: Deland.

22nd February: Miami.

26th February: Akron.

27th February: Detroit.

28th February: Flint.

ON THE STEREO SCENE

New Sweet Image Wins Band First Real U.S. Constituency

By BRUCE MEYER

For a long time — longer than they were willing to admit — Sweet were far too appropriately named.

Sweet played a kind of hard rock-bubble gum blend of music — a style that left them without a constituency in the United States.

It was no problem elsewhere.

Over a period of eight years they sold 20 million records worldwide — and were regularly voted among the most popular bands in Europe.

BUT EXCEPT FOR an overly cute single called "Little Willy" a couple of years ago, their impact on the huge American market was virtually nil.

Now all of that is changed. Sweet have had two major single hits — "Ballroom Blitz" and "Fox on the Run" — in the past four months, and sales of their "Desolation Boulevard" album (Capitol ST-11395) are excellent.

Recently they were a smash success in their first U.S. appearance in Los Angeles.

There are two good reasons for the apparently abrupt change.

FIRST, SWEET HAVE finally become an all-out rock 'n' roll band. Second, and more important, they have started doing their own writing and producing for the first time.

"Fortunately in America," says drummer Mick Tucker, commenting on the change in image, "A lot of people have latched onto 'Desolation Boulevard' — and before that, to the 'Little Willy' album — and we got a sort of a cult following out of it. Luckily, they've forgotten that we were once another sort of a band."

That "other sort of band" amounted to being a front group for a couple of talented but gimmicky songwriters named Nicky Chinn and Mike Chapman. For most of their lengthy and successful career Sweet played nothing but Chapman-Chinn tunes — and as a result made no significant impact on the American audience.

NOW IT'S ALL changed.

Sweet are doing their own material — and suddenly the New World is opening up to their music.

As guitarist Andy Scott puts it, "The musicianship was always there, but it was a matter of developing our own writing."

"Desolation Boulevard" is a kind of "greatest hits" collection for Sweet; virtually all the tracks have been successful elsewhere in the world. Side one of the album including "Ballroom Blitz" is all Chapman-Chinn. Side two including "Fox on the Run" is all Sweet. Thus what the LP lacks in cohesiveness it makes up for with variety.

"ALL THE CUTS were recorded at different times in different places," says bassist Steve Priest, defending the album's loose structure. Sometimes it even seems that they were recorded by different bands.

A cut called "A C D C" sounds exactly like the British group Slade. And, there are powerful hints of the Who, the Beatles and a variety of boogie groups like Status Quo to be found elsewhere in the collection.

So although they now seem to be on the right track, it's not exactly downhill from here for Sweet. A lot will depend on the overall success of the rather bumpy tour that followed that big gig on the West Coast — and on the reception given their fine new single, "Action," and a forthcoming album, "Give Us A Wink."

29th February: Grand Rapids.

4th March: Brown County Arena, Green Bay, Wisconsin.

5th March: Civic Centre, St Paul, Minnesota.

6th March: RKO Orpheum, Davenport, Iowa.

7th March: Kansas City, Kansas, Memorial Auditorium.

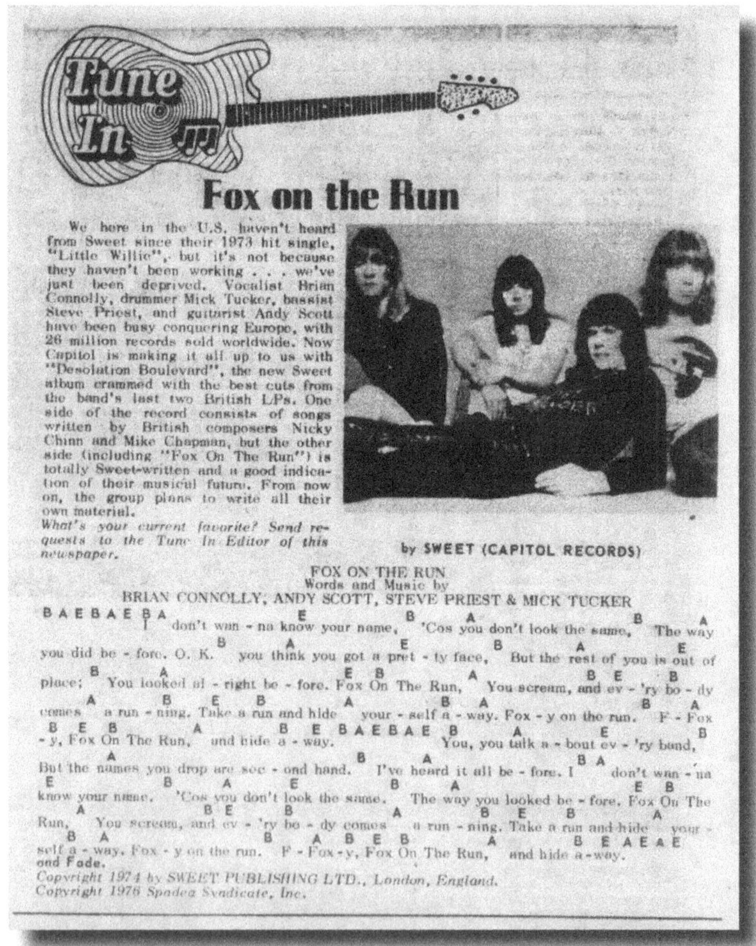

Fox on the Run

We here in the U.S. haven't heard from Sweet since their 1973 hit single, "Little Willie", but it's not because they haven't been working . . . we've just been deprived. Vocalist Brian Connolly, drummer Mick Tucker, bassist Steve Priest, and guitarist Andy Scott have been busy conquering Europe, with 26 million records sold worldwide. Now Capitol is making it all up to us with "Desolation Boulevard", the new Sweet album crammed with the best cuts from the band's last two British LPs. One side of the record consists of songs written by British composers Nicky Chinn and Mike Chapman, but the other side (including "Fox On The Run") is totally Sweet-written and a good indication of their musical future. From now on, the group plans to write all their own material.

What's your current favorite? Send requests to the Tune In Editor of this newspaper.

by SWEET (CAPITOL RECORDS)

FOX ON THE RUN
Words and Music by
BRIAN CONNOLLY, ANDY SCOTT, STEVE PRIEST & MICK TUCKER

I don't wan-na know your name, 'Cos you don't look the same, The way you did be-fore. O. K. you think you got a pret-ty face, But the rest of you is out of place; You looked al-right be-fore. Fox On The Run, You scream, and ev-'ry bo-dy comes a run-ning. Take a run and hide your-self a-way. Fox-y on the run. F-Fox-y, Fox On The Run, and hide a-way. You, you talk a-bout ev-'ry band, But the names you drop are sec-ond hand. I've heard it all be-fore. I don't wan-na know your name, 'Cos you don't look the same. The way you looked be-fore, Fox On The Run, You scream, and ev-'ry bo-dy comes a run-ning. Take a run and hide your-self a-way. Fox-y on the run. F-Fox-y, Fox On The Run, and hide a-way. and Fade.

Copyright 1974 by SWEET PUBLISHING LTD., London, England.
Copyright 1976 Spadea Syndicate, Inc.

10th March: La Crosse, Wisconsin, Marye Sawyer Auditorium.

11th March: Riverside Theatre, Milwaukee, Wisconsin.

12th March: Ambassador Theatre, St Louis, Missouri.

Southern rock

Lynyrd Skynyrd, Outlaws turn Winterland into Dixie

Lynyrd Skynyrd and The Outlaws playing San Francisco was no ordinary event. One could tell because Bill Graham had decorated Winterland's backstage to look like a western set with hay on the floor and a backdrop of the sheriff's office and the general store.

It was in honour of these two groups, who sold out Winterland almost three days running. There was even an authentic, stinky mule called Pandora there Friday and Saturday night.

After a superb and invigorating performance by The Outlaws, Lynyrd Skynyrd entered to the blasting of "Double Trouble" from their new album, "Gimme Back My Bullets."

The six-piece group is one of the hottest southern boogie bands and hails from the same part of the country that brought us the Allman Brothers and Marshall Tucker.

Their first three lps were trailblazers of chugging guitars and Greg Allman-inspired drawls, and their fourth album will go gold if just from force of habit.

With the exception of the title tune, "Double Trouble," and "Searching," their fourth album is downright boring. Ronnie Van Zant's montone is fine on the hot, seething numbers, but on the slower numbers, all of which sounds very similar, his voice becomes tedious.

Fortunately, in concert this all changes. The melodies come alive and every tune is ultimately sped up. Ronnie Van Zant's voice carries over the two guitars to the back of Winterland and probably across the street. More importantly, it is perfect for their type of music. Even the boring tunes on the album (such as "All I Can Do Is Write About It") are transformed into contagious, high-powered stuff in concert.

The audience reponded with southern yells of "whooo Wee!" and repeated calls of 'Let's Boogie.' Their rousing 55-minute set concentrated on material from the new album ("Cry For The Bad Man," "I Got The Same Old Blues," "Searching," "Gimme Back My Bullets," "All I Can Do Is Write About It.") but also played old favorites like "Saturday Night Special" and "Sweet Home Alabama," on which the Confederate flag dropped down behind them.

For an encore they came back with their classic "Free Bird" from their first album, and a hokey Jimmy Roger's tune "T For Texas, T For Tennessee."

been able to break into the American market. This was and is the case with scores of British acts, recently with Gary Glitter, Alvin Stardust, Suzi Quatro, Slade, T. Rex, and the Bay City Rollers (though for the Rollers their luck may be changing. "Money Honey" is a hit and they are tentatively planning a U.S. tour).

Very few groups actually make it in America and Sweet, a young punk English group is coming closer than most. Last year they had two gigantic hits, first with "Ballroom Blitz," followed by "Fox On The Run," and now "Action."

With a total of 26 million record sales worldwide and some enthusiastic reviews, people are beginning to take them seriously.

Sweet did a trial run at Santa Monica Civic Auditorium, sold out, and so is embarking on a major tour with their fingers crossed.

Incidentally, their date here at Winterland was canceled and no reason was given. Low advance ticket sales?

They attack their music with the same heavy metal with the hits writing duo Chapman and Chinn. That was great for a while, for Chapman-Chinn gave them 12 hits ("Little Willy" and "Ballroom Blitz" were the ones heard here) but also tagged them as a "teenybopper" band.

Now they write their own material — "Fox On The Run" was the first — and are trying to lose the reputation as just a singles band and the "Tennybopper" stigma.

Someone once termed their music "bubblegum Led Zeppelin" and it's an apt description. Just listen to "Cockroach" on their new disc "Give Us Wink."

The attack their music with the same heavy metal style and Brian Connolly half-screams over top like a spirited, though less versatile, Robert Plant.

Mick Tucker (drums), Andy Scott (lead guitar), and Steve Priest (bass) add the high harmonies and keep a snarling rhythm section.

With "Desolation Blvd." (an American disc which combines their last two English records) and "Give Us A Wink" doing well they shouldn't have any trouble establishing themselves as a legitimate hard rock band. None of the "kid stuff," rather "teen stuff" for these boys.

They are off to blitz the world, starting with America, and with their high rock n' roll, and three strong albums, they just might get the sweet success they are after.

EVAN HOSIE

"Give Us A Wink"
Sweet (Capitol Records)

In the last five years bands which are superstars in England, sell thousands of records and sell out the biggest halls, are still unheard of in America.

Even under the cover of a heavy publicity campaign, most of the hugely successful groups in England haven't

THE CLUBS
The Longbranch: San Pablo Avenue and Dwight Way: Les Dudek with Backroad, Friday, Les Dudek with Jerry Miller, Saturday.
Keystone Berkeley: Shattuck and University avenues: Stoneground with Heartsfield, Friday; Terry Garthwaite with Heartsfield, Saturday.

West Dakota: 1505 San Pablo Avenue: Salsa De Berkeley, Friday, Jerry Corbett with Fred's Band, Saturday.
Savoy: 1438 Grant Ave., San Francisco: Jerry Corbett, Friday; The Moonlighters with Barry Melton, Saturday.
Winterland, San Francisco: Montrose, Cold Blood and Sammy Hagar, Friday and Saturday.

14th March: McFarlin Auditorium, Dallas, Texas.

18th March: Seattle, Washington.
Cancelled as truck did not arrive due to snowstorms.

19th March: Paramount Theatre, Portland, Oregon.

Who's rockin'
Sweet image changes

By Bruce Meyer

Daily Breeze/News-Pilot—Fri., Mar. 19, 1976 — E12

For a long time—longer than they were willing to admit—Sweet was far too appropriately named.

Sweet played a kind of hard rock-bubble gum blend of music—a style that left them without a constituency in the United States.

It was no problem elsewhere. Over a period of eight years they sold 26 million records worldwide—and were regularlly voted among the most popular bands in Europe.

But except for an overly cute single called "Little Willy" a couple of years ago, their impact on the huge American market was virtually nil.

Now, all of that is changed. Sweet has had two major single hits—"Ballroom Blitz" and "Fox on the Run"—in the past four months, and sales of their "Desolation Boulevard" album are excellent. Recently they were a smash success in their first U.S. appearance in L.A. Sweet will be back at the Santa Monica Civic, Wednesday.

There are two good reasons for the apparently abrupt change. First, Sweet has finally become an all-out rock 'n' roll band. Second, and more important, they have started doing their own writing and producing for the first time.

"Fortunately in America," says drummer Mick Tucker, commenting on the change in image, "a lot of people have latched onto 'Desolation Boulevard'—and before that, to the 'Little Willy' album—and we got a sort of cult follow-ing out of it. Luckily, they've forgotten that we were once another sort of a band."

That "other sort of band" amounted to being a front group for a couple of talented but gimmicky songwriters named Nicky Chinn and Mike Chapman. For most of their lengthy and successful career, Sweet played nothing but Chapman-Chin tunes—and as a result made no significant impact on the American audience

Now it's all changed. Sweet is doing its own material—and suddenly the New World is opening up to their music.

As guitarist Andy Scott puts it, "The musicianship was always there, but it was a matter of developing our own writing.

"Desolation Boulevard" is a kind of "greatest hits" collection for Sweet; virtually all the tracks have been successful elsewhere in the world. Side of the album including "Ballroom Blitz" is all Chapman-Chinn. Side two including "Fox on the Run" is all Sweet. Thus what the LP lacks in cohesiveness it makes up for with variety.

"All the cuts were recorded at different times in different places," says bassist Steve Priest, defending the album's loose structure. Sometimes it even seems that they were recorded by different bands. A cut called 'A.C.D.C." sounds exactly like the British group Slade. And there are powerful hints of the Who, the Beatles and a variety of boogie groups like Status Quo to be found elsewhere in the collection.

Although they now seem to be on the right track, it's not exactly downhill from here for Sweet.

—UPI

SWEET DREAMS IN AMERICA

by Linda Merinoff

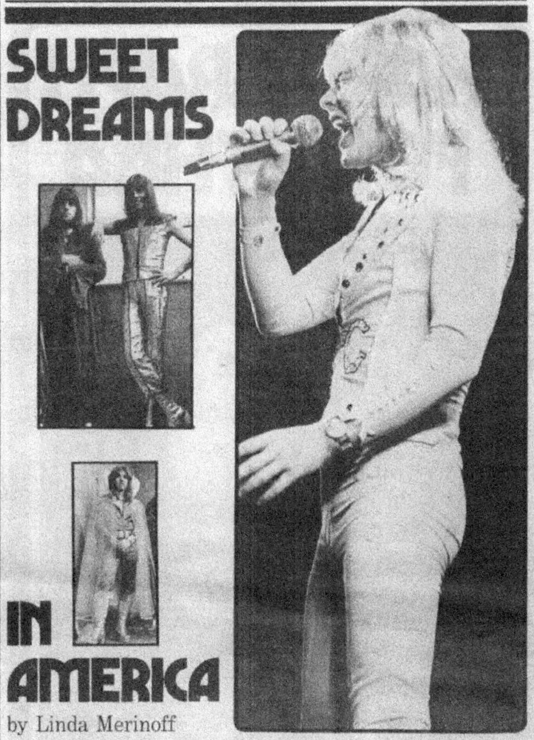

ANDY SCOTT was lounging around the dish - cluttered living room of a suite in one of New York's once - lovely hotels, the same one in which Roxy Music used to stay. Sweet were in New York for a couple of days but they won't be playing here.

Andy was eager to talk about America and he certainly should be, considering that the Sweet is one of the few English bands to have any success here at all.

"We've got to be better really, haven't we," said Andy. "Everyone says America's the hardest to break and our records have broken so we must be good. There hasn't been any hype because that way no one would have known whether it was the hype or the fact that the Americans wanted a group like us.

"We've always had a cult following in California anyway and it's amazing the amount of people who used to buy all our imports. I always considered myself lucky in terms of success, but then it doesn't become luck anymore — it's because you're really good."

"I think we're a breath of fresh air," added Mick Tucker.

"There's no one else around who's playing our particular kind of music."

"There's a lot of feel in the music, energy," said Andy. "We're the only band that doesn't have a front man really. Bands like the Yardbirds used to excite me and if we can be half as exciting as that kind of thing we're doing well."

Sweet all feel that what the American kids are looking for at a concert is lots of noise, lots of energy, real good time rock 'n' roll. They use special effects like lighting and films, but those are secondary. Although they work hard on stage, Sweet just seem to let it all happen.

Although the band's been plagued with technical problems in the first few cities like Nashville and Chatanooga they've been well received at all their dates. They've also discovered what other problems to avoid.

Andy told me: "We introduced one or two new numbers, but then there becomes a low spot and it breaks up the energy. The American kids want to be driven all night, so we're bringing back some of our old stuff."

"America's only had one album here, so we have to work within those barriers and confines," said Mick.

Afford

On this American tour Sweet are being supported by Eric Carmen, former member of the Raspberries. He is a classic pop performer, young and good - looking, and his music is vibrant enough not to turn off a Sweet audience. It's surprising that Sweet can afford to headline a tour after only two hit singles, but they seem to be selling very well.

Since they aren't playing in New York, Capitol Records hired a bus to bring people to their Philadelphia concert, about 2½ hours away. We pulled up at the Holiday Inn where we met Mick and Brian. Brian seemed all right, but Mick appeared to be very nervous, perhaps pre - concert jitters.

The concert itself went very well. The harmonies were less subtle than those on the records but still effective. The many Eric Carmen fans in the audience don't seem to be at all put off by the Sweet. Andy, however, was wrong when he said that he thought their audience in America was about 18 years old. There were very young kids in the auditorium and they seemed to be the only ones to respond, by giggling and shouting, to every vulgar comment the band made. Americans aren't used to a continual bombardment of four letter words coming down from the stage. People can get arrested here for that.

The world of Rock 'n' Roll being what it is, most of the songs the band played were from the 'Desolation Boulevard' album. All of Brian's introductions to the songs went completely over the kids' heads — not because they're so complicated but because the audience can't understand his accent.

In spite of the language barrier, most of the audience had a marvellous time, yelling, a few people in the front up dancing, the rest bouncing in their seats.

Back at the hotel suite, Andy and Mick have been speaking for about an hour. Steve and Brian wandered in and the eating and drinking began. Brian went down to the bar to see some fans who've called up to the room to say hello.

Sweet will make it in America simply because they're playing good music and they have the sensitivity to keep in touch with what their audience is looking for — even if it doesn't particularly suit the band.

That's professionalism and that's what usually wins out over here.

Wednesday 24th March: Civic Auditorium, Santa Monica, California.

Prior to this gig I rang my wife Pat to give her our flight details as it was the very last gig of the tour. This show opened with Sammy Hagar followed by Sweet. Free's Paul Kossoff had just died (19th) and the band did a version of 'Alright Now' with Ritchie Blackmore. Yes Ritchie Blackmore, got up on stage for, in his words "a blow" in Sweet's last number. Wow now it was so damn cool. Very nice guy to be with. It was a wonderful evening. After the gig we loaded the gear into two trucks, quick drink in the room and bed at 03:15am.

16 20 . Pt IV—Fri, Mar. 26, 1976   Los Angeles Times

AT SANTA MONICA CIVIC

Sweet—The Second Time Around

BY ROBERT HILBURN
Times Pop Music Critic

The Sweet, the English rock band whose U.S. debut last September at Santa Monica Civic Auditorium failed to reflect fully the infectious, tenacious spirit of its AM-oriented singles, returned to Santa Monica Wednesday night for a second try.

Seasoned by a lengthy cross-county tour, the quartet played with more bite and aggressiveness than last time but the results still fell noticeably short of the expectations set by such enormously appealing hits as "Ballroom Blitz," "Fox on the Run" and "Action."

The Sweet, it now seems clear, is a band whose music is better heard on radio than in concert. The group simply lacks both the authority and charisma on stage to add any substantial information and/or flavor to what it has already put on record.

Where that live deficiency may not have been a problem at one time in rock, the emphasis these days on theatrics—from Kiss and Queen to David Bowie and Roxy Music—causes the Sweet's lack of character and definition on stage to put the band in a difficult position.

It's not that the foursome (Brian Connolly on vocals/keyboards, Mick Tucker on drums, Steve Priest on bass, Andy Scott on guitar) didn't employ its own theatrics. Indeed, the group used film, bold thunderbolts of light and smoke screens, among other special effects. It also tried to operate from a fierce, rebellious stance.

But the effects were so elementary and the stance so unconvincing that they simply detracted from the group's impact. Despite occasional solo instrumental attempts, the band's playing was not inspired.

Without a stronger showcase for its music, then, the Sweet is in the rare position of putting the burden on the audience to comb through the weaknesses in the band's presentation to find the acknowledged values in the group's music. The fact the audience responded strongly at times Wednesday pointed up the power and appeal of the largely punk-rock music.

The fact is, however, the Sweet's music might be more enjoyable in an auditorium if someone simply played the group's records—which are filled with the kind of atmosphere and spirit that sparks one's imagination—rather than bringing the band on stage where its weak presentation tends to narrow that same imagination.

Thus, one finds himself in the somewhat ironic position after the show of driving home from a concert he didn't like, but hoping to hear one of the group's records on the radio. Odd.

Sammy Hagar, the former lead singer with Montrose who now fronts his own high-energy, hard-rock quartet, opened the show Wednesday as a substitute for Backstreet Crawler. While his voice, moves, material (some of which he wrote) and arrangements all seem perfectly acceptable by commercial measurements, the degree of originality and/or musical vision was far less than his new album title ("Nine on a Scale of 10") would suggest.

Thursday 25th March: Left for home.

I put all these concerts in, from this tour, as to me, it was the most upbeat, memorable tour we ever did...

And although I mixed with the band at home, when we were on tour it was a very different scenario because we were setting up and taking down for many hours and the band were headed straight back to their hotel. It was full on…

Friday 9th April: Myself and the crew went to Heathrow airport in a large, hired truck to collect all the bands equipment from Customs now that it had been cleared. We took it all back to our warehouse in Staines, Middlesex.

Thursday 22nd April: Myself and the crew went to Pinewood Studios where the band had been rehearsing for a couple of days and realised there had been a burglary, and some of the equipment had been stolen (about £3,000 worth). We phoned security, CID etc.

NEWS-PILOT San Pedro California Sat., Mar. 27, 1976 B2

How sweet can a hot dog be?

By Rex Dalton

As a recording group, Sweet may have proved itself by its world-wide success.

But its performance at the Santa Monica Civic Wednesday night showed them to be another hot dog rock and roll band which leaned heavily on distorted levels of volume and stage tricks to compensate for expertise.

Playing mainly cuts off its "Desolation Boulevard" album, the band played a controlled but lacking performance.

It was lacking because the four-member group sounds like a studio band playing cuts dominated by superficial melodic and verbal phrasing.

No amount of volume, gadgets or light shows will compensate for the lack of proficient rock and roll.

I refuse to believe rock and roll is based on or helped by this rank brand of Pavlovian garbage.

If Sweet has any intention of leaving its past of recording the Chinn-Chapman influenced tunes (deficient in even the most modest terms of diversity) behind them and developing a repertoire which shows they are capable of writing and playing music with depth, it wasn't evident at the concert.

The band played its hit "Ballroom Blitz," "Fox on the Run" and to an ardently near full house.

They also played "A.C.D.C.," "No You Don't" and "Set Me Free" off the "Oesolation Boulevard." They did some newer compositions, the best being "Restless" by bassist Steve Priest.

But none of these songs has any real substance. The lyrics of "Action," for instance, enhanced by the wavering screaming of Brian Connolly standing at stage center waving his arm in some maladroit political gesture, only made me want to seek refuge in the lobby.

When the band members took their solo turns on the shallow confines of their music was even more evident.

Guitarist Andy Scott, during an extended solo, played only a few bars of clean, crisp riffs with clarity. However, when ex-Deep Purple guitarist Ritchie Blackmore joined the band on the Free tune "All Night Long," and on the second and last encore, his playing was concise and articulate.

When drummer Mick Tucker took his turn in the spotlight two screens rolled down behind his elevated platform and motion pictures of him playing steel kettle drums and various percussion instruments were shown.

The audio would then vacillate between his live playing and recordings of his playing of film, with the live and tape performances combined at times.

Although this trick was synchronized quiet nicely, it appears to me to be counter productive to live performances.

People pay money to see artists perform live, not a duel between themselves and a tape.

Traced some replacement gear at various music stores and carried on rehearsing. I had forgotten all about this until I referred to my diaries to write this book.

P.S Not all the tours are in this book. Individual items from tours that were very interesting or very funny will have portions in to make you smile, roar with laughter... or just grunt!

Page 16 SOUNDS June 19, 1976

Sounds girl in Sweet nude bathing horror

*That's not **exactly** true, but it's the kind of headline we were hoping for when we sent the nubile VIVIEN GOLDMAN to join Sweet on their latest rampage across Germany. Actually she **did** strip off . . .*

THE ERSATZ raunch, bump and grind of 'The Stripper' blares out over the Sportshalle in Cologne.

Thousands of minute German teenyboppers are creaming in excitement at seeing four would-be punk yobbos from Middlesex, tell it like they think it is.

The film show is explicitly designed to get 'em going. Right and left hand screens run out-of-synch images of pop eroticism; bananas unpeel, naked kneeling girls dissolve into numerals. An obscenely red, rough, tongue licks incessantly round and round gloss-red lips, the shapes and symbols of S-E-X are displayed with dogged determination. Cabaret time, alright. Dry hump city.

"Don't worry," says curly-topped Richard Ogden, the publicist who's steering the little jaunt, "this is what you do. See?"

His body suddenly droops in a neanderthal slump, his head twitches back and forth like a crazed, disjointed robot, his shoulder heaves in some vague relation to the melody.

"See?" He snaps upright with a cheery grin. "'S easy. And when a guitar solo comes up, this is what you do."

Slumping dramatically, he picks at an invisible guitar with spasmodic jerks and knee shakes.

Could such things be?

Yup, they could. Look about, and as far as the eye can see, the cream of Germany's youth (or at least the ones with a fiver to spare for the ticket) are twitching plucking and nodding with the furious abandon of acolytes at some shrouded shrine of dark mysteries.

The reason why they're all going apeshit is because with a dramatic flourish THE SWEET are onstage, with their glorious motto 'WINKING WILL MAKE YOU GO BLIND' still emblazoned on all our minds. Well mine, anyway.

What in goodness do they make of all these excitements to depravity? Especially couched in finglish locker-room argot?

Lots and lots, it would seem.

I'm checking out this nine-year old girl next to me, niftily turned out in a matching denim waistcoat and well-cut little jeans. She's sitting on an equipment case next to me, giggling with her pal. Something her friend whispers makes her laugh out loud. She checks herself, and quickly *creases herself*, eyes dropped demurely. A split second later she's standing in front of me, expertly twitching her lips and flouncing her hair from behind, in lusciously simulated passion.

She's only the first to move. The Sweet definitely do not play body music; my favourite kind, but they do genuinely sweat it, sending waves of hard-working energy out to the scattered audience in their 'Sweet' T-shirts, 'Sweet' shoulderbags.

I mean, with all that EFFORT aimed straight at your solar plexus, you've got to do *something*, haven't you? Otherwise you're not even *trying*, I mean to say.

Sony Watson-Taylor and I look grimly at each other. With a determination that should make the National Union of Journalists proud, we pick our way through the writhing youngsters to the side of the stage, to a clear patch of ground. Amid the flying shreds of 'Pop' magazine eddying round our ankles, we gingerly twitch our necks.

We're gonna get it on.

The Sweet's dressing room, Sportshalle, Cologne. Avant-gig . . .

"RIGHT, I'm ready for battle," Sweet vocalist, front man, and token blondhair, Brian Connolly, is cheery. He's about to doff his regulation patched denims for his regulation satin tight, tight trousers — not in my presence, I hasten to assure you.

"Off with the jewellery."

Off come the chunky gold rings, the expensive no-numeral watch, the strange gold bracelet with the birth sign (Libra I think) ("I bought this 'cos they told me gold was better than keeping the money. Cost me (insert astronomical sounding sum with 4 or 5 noughts.)" That's good, Brian. If times get rough you can always flog it. "No (shocked) I'd never do that. I'll leave it to me kids. Or somebody.")

"Spot the stripper!" yells out drummer Mick Tucker breezily from across the room. It was an omen of the deadly catchphrase that was to haunt the next three days.

The Sweet's Dressing Room, Sportshalle, Cologne, Apres-gig . . .

"WADDYA MEAN you had a good hop?" Brian Connolly's not tall, but he's suddenly grown about ten inches. His eyes, normally slightly glazed and red, shoot steely blue.

"You meantasay you were DANCING while we were up there sweating our bloody BALLS off!"

What can I say? I meant it as a compliment, and I've committed the unpardonable crime of bopping. Obviously a major faux pas. Desperately I say, "Well, it was just meant to show appreciation of the music, y'see . . . it makes you feel good so you want to dance to it."

Suspiciously, Brian growls, "Don't know what you mean. Music doesn't make me wanna dance. Funk makes me want to play." Aha, but that's because you're a musician while I am but a humble scribe, you honour. If I could play, maybe it would make me want to play too.

"Oh, I see," Brian is obviously thinking. Lines furrow his brow.

"You . . . mean that you're dancing to express what you feel about the music?"

Well, that is the general idea. Yes.

"Oh. Well, in that case it's alright. We're in agreement."

Jovially, he pats me on the shoulder and walks away.

The lobby of the Intercontinental Hotel, Cologne. Apres-gig . . .

"TWO BIRDS went for 'im, and I'm afraid it 'ad to be a bit of that." It's a member of the Sweet's entourage ex-

Pix: Dennis Morris

June 19, 1976 SOUNDS Page 17

pounding to a sympathetically nodding colleague. They're both looking in the direction of an emphatic German madwoman who looks about 14. She's causing some kind of rumpus over at the desk, insisting that she's staying with a friend in the hotel, hanging at the phone. This, apparently, is the Fan Who Came Too Close. Having the dubious privilege of being the last fan to break Brian Connolly's back, she's now making a vain attempt to entrench her position.

'Yeah, 'cos in Denmark all my fuckin' forehead was scratched open . . .'

'Yeah,' agrees his mate solemnly, 'he belted her one.'

They all gaze solemnly at the Fan, who's vigorous as ever.

'She's not complaining,' they all agree. 'She's just trying to bullshit.'

I'm feeling faintly relieved, patting myself on the back that Connolly and I wound up in agreement. Plastic surgery ain't that easy to get on the N.H.S.

The Europa Bar, apres-gig. Later.
THE BAND are taciturn, laidback, knocking back the booze with an easy, regular elbow motion that confirmed what one of the guys had said to me earlier — 'We're not a drugs band.' Too right, sailor.

All of a sudden some sixth sense warns me that Andy Scott, the dark guitarist who looks just like Mick Tucker, drummer, wants to *talk*. Seize the moment, I say grimly to myself, and squeeze in between Suzy W-T and Scott. Andy talks. At length. He's in the twilight zone of exhaustion and post-gig reaction, with post-natal depression. He wants to talk. He does.

'The fans on the road here, it's not like in England, (imitates) 'Ooh, in 'oo lovely, look at 'im.' I'm not against that, I love playing in England, but you can see what we're up against. We've still got a few younger ones there.

'But in Germany, that's like our audience and that is virtually the same audience as in America, the majority of them are 16-20. Now obviously we want to appeal to the 14's and 15's, but that majority is 16, and perhaps 21. By the time you get to 16 you must be thinkin', you've got to know what you like . . .'

He looks enquiringly at me.

The dressing room, Sportshalle, Cologne. Apres-gig . . .
BRIAN's turning on me menacingly. 'I like to make journalists feel uncomfortable. Why are you here?'

The Europa Bar, apres-gig. Later.
ANDY SCOTT (talking about rock press reaction to the Sweet's albums):

'Like we *should* be able to talk to people like from the music papers when ever we fancy, not 'cos there's a product to try and push . . . I don't see that side of the business.

'The band has put itself out too much in the past to try and help people and got shit on, so no more are we putting ourselves out. If it 'appens it 'appens. It 'appened in America that way. There was no overkill publicity. 'Ballroom Blitz' took three months to get in the charts, and when it got there it was there for a year. 'Desolation Boulevard' has been in the charts for 45 weeks.

'It's really unfair to start putting us in a retrogressive mood to start with. And really, once that attitude's in your head, you do a press reception . . . we have press receptions where we accept gold discs and shuffle out of there as quickly as possible . . . we don't even want to talk to the press . . .'

You're not doing too badly at the moment.

'I don't mind talking to people as long as they're intelligent.'

LIKE I said, the Sweet may be many things, but body music they ain't. Bob Marley eases himself down from a gig by smoking and dancing himself almost to oblivion, over the edge.

The Sweet lock themselves in their dressing-room and fight.

Suzy, Dennis Morris the Rastaphotographer, Richard and myself are slumped outside the dressing-room, B-O-R-E-D. On the floor. I'm reading Suzy's historical novel. It's awful. The band are shouting. Half an hour later, they emerge, invigorated.

'Right, we're off then.'

The Europa Bar, later . . .
ANDY SCOTT: 'If you're not into the humour of the band . . . Like, people in the press are like let inside where other people wouldn't be. Like we've had people with us who've heard us arguing . . . but they've got to realise that that is under, like, the cloak of secrecy, when you hear a band doing that.'

THE NIGHT has worn on, and all the adrenalin's ebbing away fast. It's about 4.00 a.m. I'm allowing myself one last bop on the deserted dance floor (the DJ's an exile from Notting Hill Gate. He likes reggae. The Germans don't) when a couple of girls hail me to a table. I walk over.

One's German, the other's English. The English one addresses me.

'Do you know them? The Sweet?'

I wouldn't say I actually know them yet, but I am out here with them.

'What are you doing?' I've been sent out by SOUNDS to do a story on the band.

'Oh, a journalist!' Relieved, she smiles at her friend. 'We're journalists too. Out here on a story. No, I can't tell you which one, it would spoil it. The story. Do you know which room number they're staying in?'

THE NEXT morning, a motley crew gather in the lobby. Everyone looks rather the worse for wear. Steve Priest hasn't made it downstairs yet. The rest of us crowd into the bus, and Brian and Andy shout at the driver. He really was a lousy driver, mind you.

Dennis almost decapitates himself trying to get relaxed, cruisin' shots. Suzy and I compare notes (she's here for a German paper). We arrive at the airport, disembark. I knock back black coffee while the 4-foot pink stuffed donkey, a gift from a fan, is weighed at the luggage desk. Mick strolls up, and shouts cheerfully, 'Spot the donkey!' The two girls from last night sweep before us onto the plane.

A PLEASANT, refreshing day off has been enjoyed by all. Suzy slept, the band hung out, and I almost got arrested on the East Berlin border, trying to get a far-out interview with the support band, Mr. Big.

Dennis and I get lost and increasingly bad-tempered as we try and find the Sweet's hotel. Finally we make it and sink into the restaurant.

There the Sweet, who are nice blokes individually, sink into the kind of spiritual and intellectual morass that can surely only come when an all-male rock band is on the road. Even the civilising influence of Suzy and myself does little to restrain the barrack-room humour (HOW many times did it wrap round a lamp-post?) and hail of bread rolls. Decadent Berlin niteries ('even when the took her G-string off you could hardly tell, but . . .') are academically discussed. They forget to bring Suzy's order. I fall asleep at the end of the table.

THE LAST DAY before our return. I sleep all afternoon. Dennis toddles off to take pics, and Brian explains why he's decided not to buy a Rolls Royce when he already has a perfectly adequate Mercedes.

The gig goes down well that night. Pretty much the same set as before, but tighter. That night I notice gangs of little boys all kneeling in a circle on the floor, bent back from the waist, *banging their heads against the floor* beyond their feet.

There's a little apres-tour party at the swimming-pool in the hotel. We hustle past the crowds to the limo. Apparently after we leave the fans break down the plate glass doors to get at the dummies of the group.

The Party . . .
THE RECORD execs are determined to make it a night to remember, throwing girls in the pool and laughing uproariously. I slide into the water in my Marks and Spencers underwear, seeing as how nobody had told me about the athletic aspect.

Paddling furiously up and down the pool, I raise the ol' head above water for a split second, just long enough to hear Andy Scott yell, 'Spot the bra and pants!' By this stage of the game a rapport has been established between the band and me and Suzy.

Steve Priest has split, he's not much of a party man. Andy and Mick Tucker are being very amiable and chatty, even Brian has a smile. They're all relieved the trip's over, I think, and they can head on back to the family and the homestead in the stockbroker belt. Andy tells me about his plans for a house extension. I wish I had more money. I leave when the Sweet enter into the party spirit and begin flinging lofty-dressed girls into the pool.

Adieu to the Sweet. The Airport, Berlin . . .
STEVE PRIEST finally shows up, and turns out to be a good bloke. I look around for the two girls I met in the bar, half expecting to see them. Apparently they've flown everywhere the band have flown, gone to all the gigs, sending notes of admiration backstage and harrassing the road crew, just to get to their idols. They never succeeded. That's showbiz. I recall a high spot of the Sweet's act — with a resounding clash of drums, Brian announces as the band follow with their immaculate back-up harmonies, 'If we don't fuck you then someone else will.'

Dennis is looking pleased that he won't be stared at in the street in a couple of hours — you'd think he was Brian Connolly or someone, the way heads turned in the street at the sight of his natty, natty dread-locks. He was virtually the only non-Aryan we saw in Deutschland. Brian is very chatty on the plane, turning round in his seat to discuss this and that and feed me cigarettes.

'I do like gold discs that I can put on the wall and stare at endlessly. They mean the world to me,' Brian intones solemnly, with a twinkle in those once-steely blue eyes. Incidentally, judging from his eyes, he's in a lousy physical shape.

Richard Ogden (who's been a source of mirth all through the lowest points of the trip. They ought to write a song about me, Suzy, Richard and Dennis on this trip and call it. Someone saved my life tonight . . .) turns to me and whispers, 'You know Brian's joking, don't you?' I think he was, actually.

Farewells at the airport, London. Dennis gets held up at customs for ages while they go through all his cameras suspiciously. Sometimes being a rasta has its disadvantages. Suzy drives us back into town with Toots blaring on the cassette.

The Sweet Story as told to me by Andy Scott
'I'VE BEEN in probably three bands who've come close to nearly breakin' through. I was in a band called the Elastic Band,

Continued next page

Sweet strip

• *From page 17*

which was like a well-known circuit band, all over England but never quite broke through. In time I reckon we might have done it . . .

"Then I backed the Scaffold for a long time with Andy Roberts and a few other people. Then I was in a band called Mayfield's Mule which had a record which got into the Top 50, you know, EMI spent a lot of money . . . The band was too into the wrong kind of things, the dope counted more than the music and I couldn't handle that.

"I'd been with so many heavy-type bands I just went looking for refreshment, and I met Sweet. I'd heard a couple of their earlier records and I thought, 'I don't know if my head will *let* me handle this. Just from the record angle.

"But when I got to rehearsal, Brian wasn't there, only Stevie and me, and we just started blowing and I realised straightaway that you shouldn't take things at their face value. I was no better a player than Mick and Steve and vice versa, we all had something going for us, we all seemed to fit.

"It was like a breath of fresh air for all of us. We were all into the same kind of music, and I played them a couple of things I'd written and they just sort of fell into it straightaway, which was great.

"I remember the first gig, I knew we were winning, at one of those cloth cap clubs in Manchester, we were taken off after half an hour because we were too loud.

"At that time we were doing about a quarter original material, and a couple of Free numbers, a medley of Who tracks. Then I remember we all went up to Chinn and Chapman's office, and they played me a tape, like what I consider to be a demo tape of that 'today's sound', and I said yeah, fine. But I didn't think that that was necessarily a good direction, but I thought, it's a hit record.

"And I think we were all like over-anxious to at least see some bloody success in this business. And when it was suggested, a record company was found from somewhere and it was suggested that it be released. But none of us complained.

"We said, 'Well, if it doesn't go it doesn't go anyway and we can always try something new, something closer to where we *really* want to go.'

"And it was a session record."

And pauses. Continues.

"And I remember thinking, I've heard about things like this but I never thought we'd be involved with it."

"And so the record was a hit. And once you get yourself into that kind of mode it's . . . Like, another song was played to us and Mick and I DETESTED it. But we decided to give it a go and went in the studio and did it. And this time the backing track was laid, but we did a few things on the track.

"And it was starting to get to us there and then. Like, 'other people playing on my bloody record? No way!' That's why the B-side was such a contrast to *their* music, the A-side. It was our only outlet. And it was the first thing we demanded.

"By then we'd had two hit records. That's usually when all the problems start with a band, especially if you've got strong musical feelings like Mick and I had.

"We used to leave tracks like 'Blockbuster' so raw when we left the studio. But when we heard the final mix thing of it, it'd been neatened up, and instead of being something raw, it became, you know . . .

"After 'Ballroom Blitz' I thought, you know, that's it, we're not going in the studio with nobody else, we'll get it together ourselves. When they mixed it and fed that tape of some kids chanting in, I couldn't 'andle that. It became a contrived thing in the end. We had musical arrangements control, but none on the final product or how it was presented.

"In the end we went in with Phil Wainman and said, 'Alright, that's it, let's get an album together'. And we did 'Sweet Fanny Adams'. But we were still a little bit frightened to go the whole hog.

"There are parts of that album which were a bit contrived, had to be. With 'Desolation Boulevard' we tried to go for a wide-type feel to the album within the studio framework. You wouldn't believe how screwed up the guitar sound was, it was like coming out of a little hole in the corner of the speaker, and I was disgusted. RCA grabbed it and pressed a hundred thousand before we knew where we were. And that was it. The straw that broke the camel's back.

"We went into the studio to make music, to be bastardised."

After that point, the Sweet started looking after their own. 'Fox On The Run' followed, their first non-Chinnichap single, and hit. Now they're on their own, the lads who Andy described to me as "probably one of the straightest rock 'n' roll bands around."

Like Ogden told me before we left, the Sweet are big in Germany.

London Airport
MICK TUCKER comes up to me. "When's your article coming out?" Coupla weeks I guess, Mick. "Well, I'm gonna read it, and if it's nasty I'm gonna get you!" With a light laugh, he heads on home.

The end

Interesting moments as 1976 went on…

Saturday 17th July: My wife, Pat and I went to Mick Tucker's birthday party (29 today). Chatted with him, nice drinks, buffet etc. Very enjoyable. Got home at 3:00am.

Monday 19th – Friday 23rd July: Went with equipment and some crew to Ramport Studios (The Who's studios). I presumed we were rehearsing and recording but my diary does not go into detail.

Wednesday 28th July: Bang Martin and I went to Mick Tucker's house. He took us to a pub for a drive his new Mercedes 350 SL.

Monday 2nd – Wednesday 4th August: Rehearsing at Pinewood studios for Japanese tour.

Friday 6th / Saturday 7th August: We all left for Japan well ahead of the first show because the band wanted to do further rehearsals when they got there. We left Heathrow on a DC8, arrived in Moscow three and a half hours later for a refuel. Stayed on the plane for one hour and then took off again. Arrived in Tokyo nine and a half hours later... eight hours ahead of GMT.

The guys from Udo Artists picked us up and took us to the Hilton Hotel. Finally went to bed at 5:10 am, after being up for twenty-eight and a half hours (with only four hours sleep on the plane!)

Monday 9th August: The crew went to the airport with Ushi our Japanese tour helper and interpreter to get all the band's equipment cleared through customs.

Tuesday 10th August: The crew all went to the gig, spent all day setting up for the band to arrive at 6:15pm for their first Japanese sound check. We checked everything through until 9:00pm.

Wednesday 11th August: We all got up early and had breakfast, worked on the gear at the venue, then the band arrived and we had a long rehearsal finishing at 8:55pm.

Saturday 14th August: Ice Arena, Sapporo. Rock Festival '76. This was supposed to be the first gig in Japan but it would seem from my diary that the band before Sweet over ran its time and Sweet left with heavy scenes going on, i.e. the management arguing with the Japanese management. We packed up and went back to our hotel. All very strange.

This was so untypical in Japan. Everything else was unbelievably slick. For example, one of the most fascinating and wonderful things that happened in Japan, was the men in white coats who took measurements on the stage of where all the kit was positioned when we first set it up and replicated it at the venues on the tour.

I am not listing all the concerts here as Brad Jones has done a marvellous job in his book with that. My sole task is to fill in lots of personal bits that were interesting, funny, or usually both.

Thursday 19th August: Before the gig, in the evening, at the Sun Rhya, myself, Lindsay, Steve and Brian all went out to treat ourselves to a lovely Seiko watch each. (I have no idea where that watch is now).

Friday 20th August: Got the Bullet train from Tokyo to Nagoya (250 mile in two hours — a first then). Checked in to International Hotel. Flo and I changed and walked around the huge underground shopping arcade, dressed as Arabs and then around the hotel. Don't ask me why... I have no recollection.

Five more gigs in Japan and then we set off for home via Alaska on Sunday 28th August. Arrived in London an hour late on the 29th. All the Japanese people we met were very accommodating.

Friday 3rd September: Forward Air had loaded all our equipment onto their large truck (after UK clearance of it after arriving back from Japan.) They delivered to our storage accommodation in Staines, Middlesex and it was all carefully put away, ready to be thoroughly checked and serviced the following week.

Monday 13th September: Went to Audio International Studio with Martin Hodgson, Trevor, and Steve King and got Sweet's kit all set up for recording. This must have been for the *Off The Record* album. It would seem from my diary that we were there until 15th October. It was a great album.

Friday 15th October: The group signed a new recording deal with Polydor Records on this day.

Monday 18th October: I went into town and collected a new pair of speakers for my own stereo system at home. Yamaha NS 1000 monitors. Still have them, never failed... forty-four years. Not bad eh? They have been in approximately fourteen homes in England, USA and Mexico. And they have never gone wrong.

Sour looks from the new Sweet

I KNEW I'd blundered when I told Brian Connelly and Mike Tucker, of Sweet, that the vocal harmonies on their last album sounded very much like Queen.

"Don't you mean Queen's vocals sound very much like ours," said singer Brian, after an embarrassing silence.

It was the only sour moment in a very pleasant chat I had with Brian and Mike over dinner in Newcastle last week.

Sweet were in town on a promotional visit — the main object of which was to erase the past and talk about the very different sort of music the band are putting over now.

The group are huge on the Continent, particularly in Germany, and have recently conquered vast new audiences in Japan and America with their new Deep Purple-style heavy rock music.

But in Britain they are still remembered solely for their Chapman-Chinn commercial singles and their Top of the Pops appearances in full make-up with bass guitarist Steve Priest camping it up.

"We enjoyed the old days but it was all a sham. We used to do outlandish things on television just for a laugh. We were amazed that a lot of people used to take it seriously. Some of them still think we're all queer."

Sweet don't need the British sales — Germany, the U.S. and Japan are much bigger markets. It's a matter of pride and self-satisfaction which makes them so desperate to win musical acclaim in their home country.

They have no intention of becoming tax exiles. "We have beautiful homes and children here." Mick said. "We don't want to leave. We just want to do well here."

Ironically the first single written by the band, Fox on the Run, is their all-time best-seller with three million copies sold around the world.

It was a bridge between the old and new styles.

A new album is near completion. It was nearly all written in the studio.

The new style Sweet is in fact not new at all. They used to perform their own heavy rock stuff on B-sides of old singles.

To be honest, the last album didn't particularly turn me on, because I'm not too keen on riffy Purple-Sabbath type stuff.

But best of luck to the lads.

Friday 29th October: Collected a three-ton truck and went to Kingsway Recorders to pack up all the bands gear and take it back to the storage unit in Staines.

Monday 1st November: Martin Hodgson, road manager with Sweet for a long time (nicest cool guy) and I dropped off some of Andy's guitars at his home and he showed us his new studio extension he'd had built.

Tuesday 16th – Tuesday 23rd November: More recording at Audio International Studio for the *Off The Record* album. I have to say... this was all forty-six years ago (yes 46 years ago)! In no way shape or form does that seem possible...

During this time a bass drum fell on my big toe and burst it open (Ouch, fuck!!) — Nick (studio sound guy) took me to hospital, x-ray (all okay) and Tetanus jab.

May not sound too exciting but on the way to the studio one day, I picked Andy up and he dropped his Rolls off at HR Owen in London for a bit of tender loving care.

Saturday 11th December: Lufthansa Flight to Bremen in Germany with the band and Mick Angus. He had the patience of a saint to look after the band (or any band). We were all picked up at the airport in a Mercedes 600 limousine and headed to one of the TV studios. Dress rehearsal later in the day and finally did the show at 11:00pm, performing 'Lost Angels' on *Musikladen.*

Sunday 12th December: Back to England. Pretty much a rest period here until after Christmas in England.

1977

Brian, Andy, Steve and Mick were now in a period in their career where they were thinking more laterally, i.e., where do we go from here? To keep moving forward and up.

Not easy, because they weren't all thinking along the same lines.

Andy and Mick I would say were the driving forces at this time but naturally the other band members were involved in the discussions.

Management were also gauging the best direction from here, and however good management is, it has to work mutually but with the odd shouting match here and there to relieve the tension (all good fun looking on from the crews point of view).

The crew were not just employees they were very proud of what the band had achieved and wanted in any way they could, to offer suggestions by looking at it all from the outside perspective.

Wednesday 5th January: Limited crew and the band flew from Heathrow to Munich in Germany. According to my diary we only took the band's instruments on board the plane. British Airways, Desk 42, Flight 644 to Munich, then Mercedes 600 limousine to TV studio.

Friday 7th January: My cousin Chris, who was a manager at a Ford dealership delivered a new Ford Cortina Ghia estate in black for Martin Hodgson and myself to use for all the massive running around we were now doing to keep things running like a Swiss watch.

Monday 17th – Sunday 23rd January: Recording at Kingsway Recorders. On the 21st I went to Beckenham in London to organise personal number plates for Mick's car: 77 MTT.

Tuesday 1st – Friday 4th February: Back finishing recording at Kingsway Recorders. *Avis* had no truck available, so we collected all the equipment on the 7th.

Thursday 10th – Tuesday 22nd February: Two band things today, first I went to Brian's to collect his black Mercedes Benz 450 SLC to have new headlamp glass put in and then took it back to him.

I drove around Gerrards Cross and many other areas to all estate agents to see if there was a suitable property that the band could purchase and turn it into their own recording studio. This never happened.

Monday 28th February: Collected drums from Kingsway Recorders and took them to ITN studios in London to do a promotional film. I don't actually remember this too well.

Friday 11th March: My birthday. Just thought I would throw that in. Not much happening this month.

Monday 28th March: Went with the band and management to look at houses for a studio again. I thought they had by-passed this thought, but obviously not. But the limousine ride was lovely.

Wednesday 31st March: Martin and I went to our equipment warehouse to collect two Revox tape recorders. Took one to Andy's and one to the office.

Picked up a bone from the butchers to give my dog Wellington when I got home (a bit of normality).

The Fever Of Love (RCA PB 5011) is the Sweet's strongest single for a long time.

It has all the hallmarks of success that characterised their classic singles, like Blockbuster and Fox On The Run. At the same time, it incorporates the musical advances they have made over the past two years, which have seen them consolidating their success abroad and achieving the status of one of Britain's biggest heavy rock bands.

The Fever Of Love has a very pushing beat that drives Brian Connolly's vocals and Andy Scott's guitar through a high energy, gutsy performance that should see the Sweet establish themselves once more in the top ten.

****

For the first three weeks of April I seemed to be going to Massey Radio in Chiswick to see the owner Frank because the group were having a bit of a well-earned spending spree, up grading all their Hi-Fi systems and anything else in their homes. Good for them — they deserved it.

Thursday 28th April: Myself and two other members of the road crew spent the day at our warehouse checking all the bands equipment and cleaning Mick's drums etc.

Friday 29th April: Andy met us at the same warehouse and we all did a second check to make sure that everything was in perfect order.

Saturday 30th April: Just slipping this in. I went to my golf driving range for a workout. Bought a second-hand No.2 wood for £4.95. How times have changed.

(Arista).

Up till now, she has achieved occasional singles successes with gentle rock songs like **"Rock A Doodle Do"** and disco-orientated material such as **"It's In His Kiss"** without ever becoming an automatic chart fixture.

And she claims it is because there are so many facets to her singing

"One side of me is disco appeal, another side of me

It's a Sweet sensation

Sweet

Sweet: "Off The Record" (RCA)

NOW this band are a revelation these days. Far from being a mere thinking man's teenybopper band, they have now started to wield as much musical muscle as anyone.

And this is perhaps their most effective effort yet. Sweet have as much polish and panaché as Queen — and a lot more conviction.

Brian Connolly delivers songs like " Fever of Love " and " Midnight And Daylight " with real guts, energy, and a great sense of melodrama.

There's a lot of aural trickery for stereo freeks, and the whole album is composed of hard hitting rock music that goes ever so slightly over the top.

Great stuff

ingham band among the fortunates at the top of the heavy metal music tree.

Quite simply, it's the first time they have been convincing on an album. Basically, it's very dramatic, heavy and hits you with blitzkreig force.

Highlight for me was a version of "Diamonds and Rust", a Joan Baez song. That's right Joan Baez. Judas Priest do for it what Nazareth did for Joni Mitchell's "This Flight Tonight".

And the lengthy track "Sinner" is also punch rock music, with the force of dynamite.

In short, it should make them big names.

Quantum Jump: "Barracuda" (Electric Record Co.).

A SPARKLING second album from an accomplished British rock band with good pedigrees and a line in complex, sometimes jazzy musical patterns

Monday 2nd May: I bought VCR tapes in Chiswick for the guys. Took six to Andy's and had a nice chat about everything. Took six to Steve's and had another nice chat about everything. Steve was one of the most easy-going guys I have ever come across. Sure he had his moments but they were very low key.

SWEET CHOICE

SWEET. Off The Record (RCA): Before they disappeared from view, I read somewhere that Sweet were all — out to kill their tenny-bopper image and hit us with some meaningful rock.

Well ... not quite. I can't question the skill of guitarist Andy Scott, or even the voice of Brian Connolly. But for me, Sweet have changed little from the old days.

Monday 9th May: Went to Clearwell Castle, Gloucestershire. Upon arrival the truck with the equipment had already arrived. Set some gear up.

Off The Record was only released the month before but now they were already working on the follow up for their new label.

Tuesday 10th May: Woke up, got up, great breakfast, set more gear up. Andy and Steve arrived and we all chatted about the project. Then Mick and Brian arrived. Some of us went to check out Rockfield Studios which was fairly nearby. Got to bed at 5:35am.

Wednesday 11th May: Woke up at midday. I went into Coleford, a small town nearby with Mick Angus. I can visualise him now as if it were yesterday. A purchase was made of a set of darts and a dart board, badminton stuff etc.

Back to the castle and all played football in the huge grounds, a great way to unwind, ready to write some amazing songs.

Thursday 12th May: Long day here for Jeff (road crew) and I. We drove back to our gear warehouse in Staines where we picked up a few more pieces of gear that the band wanted. We then went to our London office to collect something. (can't recall what). Then drove back to Clearwell Castle (a nice little round trip of 289 miles) shattered.

Friday 13th May: Everyone is still getting into the right frame of mind to write some wonderful new songs. Mick let me take his Mercedes 6.3 for a spin. Yep, nice.

Friday 13th – Sunday 22nd May: The crew were not with the band during this period, they just wanted total isolation to be able to concentrate on new songs. This was good thinking.

Monday 23rd May: Martin, Trevor and myself headed back to the castle again. The band did some rehearsing and then we all went to a couple of pubs.

Now… I am not sure what this date was at Clearwell Castle but it *is* hilarious. One night Martin, Mick's drum guy came to me in my bedroom and said, "You won't believe this, but I can get into the loft from my room and walk/creep across over to Andy's bedroom" (you know where this is going?)

He said, "I have found an old chain and tonight I am going to go up there and over to Andy's room and rattle it like a ghost would". I said, "Okay then over to you". So the deed was done and well, it was so hilarious at breakfast the following morning.

Andy was telling the rest of the band that he wanted to change rooms because his was haunted. We all looked on in amazement, I honestly can't remember if Andy ever found out. I don't think so as it would have ruined it forever.

Monday 30th May: While the band was still writing songs, Andy got me to take his Rolls Royce to be washed, cleaned and polished in nearby Blakeney. I think they were thrilled to do it. This led to all their cars going there for the best clean they ever had.

So a very different period for the band to write some amazing new material for the world to enjoy.

Thursday 2nd June: Still at Clearwell Castle. This was a "get the little jobs out of the way for everybody" day. I went to Blakeney to collect Brian's black Rolls Royce which had been cleaned, vacuumed, and polished. Back at the castle I did some cleaning and checking of all the sound equipment.

Lindsay from the London office arrived and we all chatted, played cricket, archery etc. These moments could be quite inspiring for song writing, believe it or not. If you get a break from it, new melodies and ideas come into your head.

Friday 3rd June: This next bit I don't remember but my diary says that I recorded voice with Andy! Maybe I did sneak a little in on one track.

Monday 13th June: I met Andy. He was having more work done on his Rolls Royce. Took him to Tempo music store, he tried a 12-string Rickenbacker guitar and bought it. I drove Andy home.

Wednesday 15th June: All off to France to the Le Château d'Hérouville, near Pontoise near Paris. Nothing particular to report from looking at my diary except that I think they were much happier working at Clearwell Castle.

What is interesting is that Andy's friend Ritchie Blackmore had spent time at Clearwell in 1974 with Deep Purple and at the Chateau in April '77 with his own band Rainbow. Just coincidence?

Tuesday 5th July: I flew back to London for the day on Air France from Charles De Gaulle. I was picked up by Rob, the band's chauffeur and taken to our warehouse to pick up a few bits and pieces. (I am sorry, I can't remember what, but they were fine to be taken on the flight back). Later in that day I went to my son's sports day and ended up in the father's race and came sixth. (Not happy!).

Wednesday 6th July: I was picked up by Rob and headed back from Heathrow to Paris again.

Saturday 16th July: We all headed back to London... The crew and I came last via the truck on the ferry from Calais, which sailed at 2:10 am. Arrived at Dover one hour, thirty-four minutes later.

Monday 18th July: A mess... Martin and I went to Kingsway Recorders, only to find out that all the band's equipment had been impounded in Dover. We went to the band's office to collect Lindsay, and we all went to Dover. Spent the day there getting all the equipment cleared.

Problem was there were items not on the carnet that had been bought in France, there were receipts, but items not on the carnet should not have gone on the boat with all the main equipment. It turned out it was only four items but the trucks had left so we put them in the boot of the car and headed back to London.

Wednesday 20th July: I went to the band's office in London and did all my French accounts. Then Bang Martin arrived and we all discussed a new idea for a new stage set for the band. From there we went with Mick Angus, to the studio. I took Andy home early because he had fainted earlier. I honestly don't remember this, but it is here in my diary in front of me.

Tuesday 26th July: I met Trevor at our warehouse and we went to look at a larger one to give us more room for the band's equipment, but it was tatty and not suitable.

Wednesday 27th July: Myself and Trevor went to Bray Studios in Windsor, a new addition was being built which may be suitable.

Thursday 28th July: Met Trevor again at Bray Studios. We chatted to the manager and asked him to arrange a draft lease through the solicitors.

Sunday 31st July: I picked Steve up and we went to Tempo music store (private viewing). Tried basses and speaker cabinets out. Steve bought a Gibson Thunderbird bass and two Fender cabinets.

Monday 5th September: The guys were in De Lane Lea Studios, putting a track down, I believe.

Tuesday 6th September: I went to Andy's for him to try the Gibson Firebird guitar he had bought. Great choice.

Wednesday 7th September: The band were back in Kingsway Recorders, always my favourite recording studios. My diary doesn't list what they were recording.

Thursday 8th September: A day spent with the band in Germany.

Friday 9th September: All went to Badkissingen to Polydor sales convention. Sweet did a big interview and had a couple of tracks played to the sales force. Back to England in the evening. Plane delayed by an hour. Got home at 1:00am. The rest of this month was spent doing repairs on the band's equipment. E.g., fixing new grills on to the bass cabinets.

Monday 3rd October: Went to Kingsway Recorders in London to collect all their equipment after they had finished recording.

Friday 21st October: New crew car! Went to a car dealership in Weighbridge and got a part exchange on the Rover against a two-year-old Volvo 245 E Estate. Turns out David Walker had said no but the band had agreed it. I spoke with Andy and David that evening and got it all sorted out.

Saturday 29th October: Collected the Volvo 245 Fuel Injected DL automatic estate car. Nice! (Badly needed).

Monday 31st October: The alarm went off in the band's equipment storage place. Rushed over but it was a false alarm. Phew!

Tuesday 1st November: Swift start to the month! Martin, Alan, and myself went to Andy's house. We all went to the music store in Reading (Rumbelows), to try some effects pedals. Bought two and then dropped Andy at home. In the afternoon, dropped keyboards off in Frogmore to be serviced.

Wednesday 9th November: Crew put equipment in truck and we all went to the Rainbow Theatre. Got everything set up and they did a promotional film for four of their songs. Bed 1:05 am. (There were many, many late nights as you can imagine).

Friday 25th November: Jerry Hart joined the crew as the keyboard specialist. Turned out to be a lovely guy and "right on top" in looking after the keyboards side of the band.

Tuesday 29th November: Rehearsal at the "Farmyard", ensuring that all songs were rehearsed for the upcoming tour. Two extras who were brought in for touring (Gary Moberly and Nico Ramsden), were there too, and in full swing ready for touring with the band.

Thursday 1st December: The crew continued working, doing stuff through the night from the previous night. Carried on working on equipment and lots of other things that needed to be done whilst the band rehearsed. Finally got to bed at 10:15 pm (having been up and awake for thirty-seven hours! Couldn't do that now! Phew!)

Thursday 8th December: My wife and I went to Andy and Jackie's house for the evening. Had nice drinks, wonderful meal and had what I call a real chat, when there is real time to express thoughts, ideas and generally talk about things that I would normally never have time for. A lovely evening. Thanks again to both of you.

Thursday 22nd December: Sweet had an office Christmas party in the management's London office. A good time was had by all and finished at 6:00pm.

1978

Sunday 1st-Tuesday 3rd January: The year started with setting up all the band's equipment at Pinewood studios for the band to rehearse.

Thursday 5th-Monday 9th January: Band arrived. Full rehearsal for the next few days including the 9th.

Tuesday 10th January: The band went to Marquee Studios, to re-record 'Love Is Like Oxygen' which I believe is one of their best songs. This was probably to mime to on *Top Of The Pops* the following day as that was common then and stipulated by the Musician's Union. It was a compromise with some of the broadcasters who didn't want artists playing live in the studio. To get around this they played the songs live, recorded them, then mimed to the new recording on the TV shows.

Wednesday 11th January: We all went to the BBC for *Top of the Pops* to perform 'Love Is Like Oxygen', but sadly due to a BBC staff dispute, it didn't happen. All very depressed about it.

Thursday 12th-Tuesday 17th January: Rehearsals continued at Pinewood studios.

Wednesday 18th January: Went to the BBC and did *Top of the Pops*.

Thursday 19th January: Loaded all the gear back into our warehouse.

Monday 23rd January: Crew heads to France and Spain. Coach to Southampton then we all boarded a Townsend-Thoreson ferry.

January 21, 1978 SOUNDS Page 7
THERE'S 'NO MISTAKIN'
Love is like oxogen
Love is like oxigen
ve is like oxy
ve is like
Polydor
POLYDOR REFORM SCHc
SWEET

Tuesday 24th January: Drove towards Bordeaux. Arrived at the hotel and had a meal in the restaurant.

Wednesday 25th January: All left for Barcelona via Toulouse and the Pyrenees mountains and eventually arrived at the Colon Hotel at 11:30pm. All relaxed and then bed at 3:15pm!

Thursday 26th January: Got up at 11:30 am. Had snacks. Trucks still at the border! Trucks with equipment eventually arrived and we got everything set up. All done by 1:15 am. (And you thought this was an easy life?)

Friday 27th January: Went to the Nuevo Pabellon in Barcelona. Finalised set up. Show was at 10:15pm. All went well. Packed and loaded gear and headed back to hotel at 4:15 am. Yes! 4:15am.

Saturday 28th January: Woke up at 9:00am. Breakfast and then all headed for Lyons in France. Night off, thank goodness.

Sunday 29th January: All headed to Zurich in Switzerland. (We got around you know.)

Monday 30th January: Volkshaus, Zurich. For some reason I didn't put anything about this gig in my diary.

Tuesday 31st January: Sportshalle, Linz, Austria.

Friday 3rd February: Friedrich-Ebert-Halle, Ludwigshafen, Germany.

Saturday 4th February: Philipshalle, Düsseldorf, Germany.

Monday 6th February: Stadthalle, Erlangen, Germany.

Tuesday 7th February: Freiheitshalle, Hof, Germany.

Thursday 9th February: Stadthalle, Offenbach, Germany.

Friday 10th February: Musik Halle, Hamburg, Germany.

Saturday 11th February: Tvedhallen, Svendborg, Denmark.

Monday 13th February: Falkoner Theatre, Copenhagen, Denmark.

Tuesday 14th February: 388-mile trip to Stockholm (A long trip when you are tired).

Wednesday 15th February: Göta Lejon, Stockholm, Sweden.
Last gig of the tour. Loaded the truck. I am going to write the details of this bit… you can imagine how awful it was! Waited for the coach to arrive to take the band and crew back to England. Well… we left at 12:25am for Gothenburg. The coach broke down halfway with frozen diesel in the tank. Brian had to get a lift to the Police station in the next town. We all waited in the coach for three hours in minus 30 degrees' (almost unbearable). Brian got back with a guy and a tow truck. We eventually arrived at the Torline ferry with hardly a minute to spare — Phew.

Thursday 16th/Friday 17th February: On the boat, landed at Felixstowe at 10:00am. Home please.
My apologies for nothing too different or exciting in that section but this was a "full on" tour with very little down time.

Thursday 23rd February: Myself and the crew were excited today. We all went with full gear on a huge truck to the Hammersmith Odeon. Got all the gear in and set up for the band to arrive and do a very important soundcheck, which they did at 5:00pm. They left at 11:00pm. This was obviously a particularly important and prestigious gig for them.

Friday 24th February: Crew went to the gig and did final "tweaking and checking" of all the band's equipment. The gig was pretty much sold out. Brilliant show, brilliant audience. The audience was ecstatic when the band walked onto the stage (not bad after a three-year absence). I can only repeat… great show, great night.

Saturday 25th February: Went to our warehouse and met up with articulated truck and driver. Got all the gear back into our storage place.

RECORD REVIEW

Sweet have a new label

Sweet's line-up hasn't changed over the years, but their music has. Left to right: Mick Tucker, Steve Priest, Andy Scott and Brian Connelly.

WHATEVER happened to Sweet? Perhaps you don't much care after recalling their string of hit singles from a few years back. Remember such titles as "Wigwam Bam."

This was the period when their destinies were controlled by bubble gum rock songwriters Chinn and Chapman.

Eventually the group began to change their style — they actually had a good reputation as a heavy metal band before they started their chart career.

In this difficult period, they survived mainly by their popularity on the continent, while in Britain they appeared to sink without trace.

Although they were ignored here, the group went on to become a hit in America.

Now with a new label they have launched the album which they hope will put them back before the eyes of British rock. "Level Headed" (Polydor) proves that the band have a lot more talent than their previous track record suggests.

It's not a classic, but it falls in the interesting easy listening category, by ranging from slower moody tracks like "Dream On" to the synthesized, Yes-like "Air On 'A' Loop."

Unquestionably, the highlight of the disc is the current single, "Love Is Like Oxygen." The lyrics are a little corny, but it is an infectious track.

Other new albums worth a spin include:

BLACK OAK — "Race With The Devil" (Capricorn). Black Oak have a new look, a new sound and even a new name, having dropped the Arkansas and picked up four new band members. This first album from the new union with Capricorn is a perfect example of the power of the band. Outstanding tracks, apart from the title cut, include a seven-minute version of the Buddy Holly classic "Not Fade Away."

BILL BRUFORD — "Feels Good To Me" (Polydor). Drummer Bill has gathered some fine players around him for this album, which is not just a get together and blow creation. It is a series of taut, intelligent instrumentals contrasted with perhaps more accessible songs by Annette Peacock. An interesting album.

URBIE GREEN — "Senor Blues" (CTI). The title is an indication of one of the directions taken by the trombonist, whose warmth and mellowness of tone alternately powers the choruses and grabs the listener's attention with interesting solos on the Latin-styled "Ysabel's Table Dance" and the title track.

SWEET
LEVEL HEADED
ALBUM · CASSETTE
Includes The Hit Single
"Love Is Like Oxygen"
THE CONCERT
HAMMERSMITH ODEON
24th FEBRUARY

Tuesday 7th March: Martin and Alan from the road crew picked me up from home and we all went to pick Andy up.

We went to Pete Cornish's (Tech guy) to sort a few modifications out for Andy on his stage pedal board. This was something I admired about all the guys in Sweet... they wanted to move forward all of the time, with new songs, new ideas, new sounds. That's part of the recipe for success.

Friday 10th March: The permanent crew and I went to our storage warehouse. We measured all of the equipment to obtain the cubic capacity for transporting it to the USA. We were going to be leaving England on the 26th March.

Monday 13th March: Spent most of the day using a 3-ton truck to fill and take to be weighed… three times, with the truck fully loaded with different sections of equipment each time.

Friday 17th March: Meeting at Sweet's management office to go through all the final details ready to leave for the USA on March 26th.

Sunday 26th March: Depart for American tour. Went to Heathrow airport (I can still feel the excitement in me whilst I am writing this now). Got TWA 701 flight at 4:45pm on 707 aircraft to New York City. The flight took a little longer due to "stacking" over New York (now who would have remembered that if I hadn't told you.) Had taxi to Hotel Wellington, room 2542.

Monday 27th March: Day off to recuperate. Had a drink in an English pub and an Indian meal at the Mayoor Indian restaurant on W56th Street, No. 37. Bed 1:00am.

Wednesday 29th March: Onondaga County War Memorial, Syracuse.
Touring as guest band to Bob Seger. These were going to be crazy times. As you can imagine Sweet had a huge amount of equipment and special effects. This meant as soon as they had played their set, we the crew had to remove it all as soon as possible.

Thursday 30th March: War Memorial, Johnstown, Pennsylvania. Went well.

Friday 31st March: Richfield Coliseum, Cleveland, Ohio. Another great show by both bands.

Saturday 1st-Tuesday 4th April: Days off.

Wednesday 5th April: Jai Alai Fronton, Hartford, Connecticut.

Thursday 6th April: Auditorium Theatre, Rochester, New York.

Friday 7th April: Civic Centre, Baltimore, Maryland.

Saturday 8th April: Broome County Arena, Binghampton.

Sunday 9th/Monday 10th April: Houston, Texas.

Tuesday 11th April: Century II Theatre, Wichita, Kansas.

Wednesday 12th April: Civic Auditorium, Omaha, Nebraska.

Thursday 13th April: Travelling.

Friday 14th April: Coliseum, Fort Wayne, Indiana.
As you can see this was a long, very important tour for the band. They were getting fantastic audiences who were totally and utterly into Sweet.

Saturday 15th April: Riverfront Coliseum, Cincinnati, Ohio.

Sunday 16th April: Hulman Centre, Athletic Convocation Centre, Terre Haute, Indiana.

Monday 17th-Wednesday 19th April: Valuable time off for recuperation.

Thursday 20th April: Milwaukee Arena, Milwaukee, Wisconsin.

Friday 21st April: Dane County Coliseum, Madison, Wisconsin.

Saturday 22nd April: Met Centre, Minneapolis, Minnesota.

Monday 24th April: Chicago Stadium, Chicago, Illinois.

Tuesday 25th April: St John's Arena, Columbus, Ohio.

Wednesday 26th April: Athletic Convocation Centre, South Bend, Indiana.

Friday 28th April: Market Square Arena, Indianapolis, Indiana.

Saturday 29th April: Rupp Arena, Lexington, Kentucky.

Sunday 30th April: Mid-South Coliseum, Memphis, Tennessee.
As you can see this was a huge amount of concerts, travelling around a huge country, but if my memory serves me correctly, it was all quite amazing and worth every bit of it. I didn't detail any information of doing "other things" because to be honest there was no time to do anything other than relax if you had the time.

Monday 1st May: Travelled on Delta Flight 429 to Atlanta Georgia. Evening just enjoying some time out.

Tuesday 2nd May: Andy and I looked around a bookstore, then got a cab to Peaches record store and bought some albums. In the evening, Andy, Steve, Mick, Angus, Nico, Gary and I went in the Hertz car to Rosie's Cantina to watch a band play. Gary and Nico had a jam session with the band. (When you can play you wanna play!) A nice evening.

Wednesday 3rd May: Municipal Auditorium, Birmingham, Alabama.

Thursday 4th May: Centroplex, Baton Rouge, Louisiana.

Saturday 6th May: Omni Auditorium, Atlanta, Georgia.
The entire crew left at 3:00am for New York by coach.

Monday 8th May: Myself and two other crew members Jerry and Blenk, got a cab to JFK airport. Got 9:00pm Pan Am flight 102 with prepaid tickets (but standby). Nice Jumbo 747.

Tuesday 9th May: Arrived at Heathrow after a six-and-a-half-hour flight. We are home, xxx. Wow! What a tour that was then…

Thursday 25th May: Back to America. Got the TWA flight 771 (Jumbo) to Chicago (7hrs 55 minutes). Stayed at the Holiday Inn in Elk Grove Village.

Saturday 26th May: Drove to Waterloo.

Sunday 27th May: Mackeroy Auditorium, Waterloo, Iowa.
Rush did their set, Sweet did their set. All left for Wisconsin.

Monday 28th May: Alpine Valley Theatre, East Troy, Wisconsin.
Now this was an interesting one! Uriah Heep, Sweet and Rush.

Wednesday 31st May: Masonic Auditorium, Detroit, Michigan. Three bands here: Uriah Heep, No Dice and Sweet. All left for New York.

Friday 2nd June: Nassau Coliseum, Long Island, New York.
Sweet and Foghat.

Saturday 3rd June: Spectrum, Philadelphia, Pennsylvania.
Cheap Trick, Sweet and Foghat. After all the packing and loading we set off, through the night to Kingston, Massachusetts. Checked in at Howard Johnsons Hotel at 7:30 am. Bed. yes you read that right — a very, very long day.

Sunday 4th June: Civic Theatre, Providence, Rhode Island.
Now this was a fantastic, exciting and very special concert, because… Sweet, Rainbow, Atlantic Rhythm Section (they were

superb) and Foghat were all performing (and doing some of my favourite songs of the era).

These were all excellent bands, it was a lot of fun and we all felt very privileged to be involved in such an amazing gig with a line-up like this. This was followed by three days off recuperating.

Thursday 8th June: Hersheypark Arena, Hershey, Pennsylvania, Home of Hershey chocolate bars. Sweet and Foghat. Set off for Syracuse. Bed at 3:50am.

Friday 9th June: Onondaga County War Memorial, Syracuse, New York.
Sweet and Foghat. Great audience, well, all great but I had a great "feel" tonight.

Saturday 10th June: Memorial Coliseum, Newhaven, Connecticut. Sweet and Foghat. All left for Pittsburgh.

Sunday 11th June: Stanley Theatre, Pittsburgh, Pennsylvania.
Sweet (power cut out twice). REO Speedwagon.
Now we have a slight problem — Sweet started their set and hey presto the electric cut out, so off the stage they went. Power back on — the continuation started and the power went out again! Naturally the band were not happy with this situation… When fixed Sweet came back on and finished their set which was then followed by REO Speedwagon who were also a great band.

Wednesday 14th June: Warner Theatre, Washington DC.
Sweet and REO Speedwagon.

Friday 16th June: Scope Convention Centre, Norfolk, Virginia.
Walter Eagan, Sweet and REO Speedwagon.

Saturday 17th June: Civic Centre, Roanoke, Virginia.
Walter Eagan, Sweet and REO Speedwagon. The moving of so much equipment between sets, always left audiences to rest a while, have a drink, or whatever.

Sunday 18th June: Civic Centre, Charleston, Virginia.
All arrived having driven a very pretty journey from Roanoke. Walter Eagan, Sweet and REO Speedwagon. Checked in to the Holiday Inn. Relaxed and Phew… bed.

Tuesday 20th June: Civic Centre, Wheeling, West Virginia.
After the gig, a few of us went to the *Lucky Lady* club in the truck stop next door to the gig. Had a few drinks and a snack in the truck stop. Back to the hotel and bed at 4:30am.

This was the last gig of yet another successful tour of the USA.

They had a great audience as usual although nothing specific springs to mind, except the audience were thrilled, as they were wherever Sweet did any of their fabulous concerts.

Wednesday 21st June: Packed, breakfast. Went to Pittsburgh airport. Got Allegheny flight on a DC 9 aircraft to New York, La Guardia Airport. Checked in for standby flight at 8:30pm. Hung around for four hours. Boarded flight Pan-Am 102. Took off one and a half hour late, (didn't need that). Six-hour, ten-minute flight.

Thursday 22nd June: Arrived at Heathrow at 9:20am.
Phew… but worth Every moment. Well…

Wednesday 28th June: Off we go again... Went to Heathrow to get the 12:00pm flight but couldn't get on it. Waited for 4:00pm flight TW701 Tristar and flew to New York City. All the crew left that evening by road to North Carolina.

Despite the costs of trans-Atlantic flights in those days, we were kindly offered to travel home and have a break with our families to break the tour up into two parts.

Thursday 29th June: Well-deserved day off.

Friday 30th June: Coliseum, Greensboro, North Carolina.
Spent the morning sunbathing by the Hotel Howard Johnson's pool. All went to the gig and got everything set up. Sweet did their set and all went really well. Followed by Alice Cooper. Wow, what a great

show and such a lovely guy. The audience was very satisfied with tonight's concert, a wonderful evening. Drove through the night to Columbus Ohio.

Saturday 1st July: Municipal Auditorium, Columbus, Georgia. Got the gear in and set up and did the sound check. The first set was by the Michael Guthrie Band, followed by Point Blank and then Sweet finished off a wonderful evening of music.

Sunday 2nd July: Memorial Auditorium, Chattanooga, Tennessee. Sweet and Black Oak Arkansas.

Tuesday 4th July: The Coast Coliseum, Biloxi, Mississippi. Louisiana's Le Roux, Eddie Money, Sweet and Alice Cooper. An Amazing evening.

Friday 7th July: Sportatorium, Hollywood, Florida.

Saturday 8th July: Civic Centre, Lakeland, Florida, Civic Centre. Sweet and Alice Cooper.

Sunday 9th July: Was to be Jacksonville, Florida but was cancelled. I am not sure why.

Monday 10th July: Left for New York, boring. Lunch in a McDonald's. Arrived at the Wellington Hotel in New York at 6:55pm. Checked in then walked over to an English pub. Meal and drinks — drank too much really!

Tuesday 11th July: Crew members Jerry, Steve King and I got a cab to the airport. Got the 10:00am Pan-Am (747) flight home. Landed at Heathrow at 10:10pm.

Saturday 15th July: Martin Hodgson, Mick's drum technician came to collect the bands Volvo. He had just got back from the USA having had a few days "wind down" at the end of the tour.

Thursday 20th July: Went with Jerry, to TWA at Heathrow. Did some paperwork and arranged to go back at 2:00pm to customs. Checked all the gear was there and safely back from the USA.

Alan and Phil from Edwin Shirley Trucking company came and loaded all of Sweets equipment into the truck. We all had drinks and snacks in the bar. Went to Staines and met Jeff Blenkinsaw, another of Sweet's crew members. Got all of the gear safely off the container and into storage.

Thursday 17th August: Jerry the keyboard roadie / technician went to Andy's. We also went to Andy's and had coffee and chatted and played swing ball in the garden.

There was now a very quiet period. I am not sure why or the reason as it was so long ago.

September
Pretty much a down time for the band.

Thursday 19th October: Andy, his wife Jackie and their son Damian came to our house, had coffee, listened to some records.

Saturday 21st October: Went into Townhouse Studios, 150 Goldhawk Road (built in 1978 under the direction of Richard Branson).

Sunday 22nd/Monday 23rd October: Recording at Virgin Studio.

Tuesday 24th October: Went to the office to collect some working cash and, I remember this well... I collected Steve's new Ovation fretless bass that had arrived from America. Beautiful.

Wednesday 25th-Tuesday 31st October: Studio.

Wednesday 1st-Tuesday 7th and Wednesday 15th-Friday 17th November: Band recording at Virgin Studios.

Saturday 18th November: I went to Brian's house to drop off a set of headphones.

Monday 20th-Thursday 30th November: Virgin Studios.

Friday 1st-Thursday 7th December: More studio time including 3:00am finishes.

Friday 8th December: We couldn't do anything as Andy had cut one of his fingers.

Monday 11th-Friday 15th December: More studio time. Then back for the office Christmas party.

Saturday 16th December: Recording finished. The crew and I rented a truck and went to the studio to load all the equipment and took it back to the warehouse.

Sunday 17th December: Unloaded the vast amount of gear, all nice and tidy for next time.

Monday 18th December: Martin and I went to the warehouse to get guitars and Fender Rhodes and took them to Andy's. Andy wanted to write more songs.

The remainder of the month was back to everyday normality, visiting friends, shopping, family Christmas and totally relaxing. Phew… What a year!

1979

Here we go…

Monday 2nd April: This is the first thing that I have in my 1979 diary. Rehearsals start. We went to Bray Studios and got everything ready, checked and working. Band arrived and we all had lunch in the restaurant. I went to Andy's house to get some bits of equipment that he needed. Finished at 9:30pm.

Tuesday 3rd April: Studio again for more rehearsals. Jerry took me home at the end because Gary Moberly, keyboard player (a really good one, I might add at this stage) was using the crew Volvo estate.

Wednesday 4th-Monday 9th April: Rehearsals.

Wednesday 11th April: Set up gear at Townhouse Studios, ready for band to do new recording material. Tracks included Play all Night, Mother Earth, Call Me and many more.

Thursday 12th April: Cleared the remainder of the equipment, i.e. the drum riser and took it back to our storage building. Went on to the Townhouse Studios and the band recorded until around 11:00pm.

Friday 13th April: Last sessions in Townhouse Studios.

Tuesday 17th-Sunday 22nd April: Back to Bray studios for rehearsals.

Monday 23rd April: I drove to Peterborough in Cambridgeshire and ordered some more flight cases for the band.

'CALL ME'
The new single from SWEET
DISTURB
DISTURB
It takes the waiting out of wanting.
polydor
POSP 36

Tuesday 24th April: I went to Bray again and spoke to Andy about the gear we are using and what we probably also still needed.

Thursday 26th April: I went to Bray and met Murray, a crew member for Barclay James Harvest and showed him some of Sweet's older gear that they were selling.

Monday 30th April: Met Jerry at Bray studios and we worked on equipment all day.

Tuesday 1st May: All of the crew got together at Bray studio to discuss the upcoming American tour.

Tuesday 22nd May: Took all the equipment to Heathrow Airport and unloaded it at Pan Am clipper cargo.

Wednesday 30th May: Leave for American tour. Martin, Jerry and I went to Heathrow airport but couldn't get on to the first flight to New York because our visas were not ready! (don't ask, I don't remember the detail). Got a later flight TWA701 at 4.45pm (Boeing 747) to New York (7 hours). Checked into the Wellington Hotel.

Thursday 31st May: All went to Brito's Place and then did some rehearsing.

Friday 1st June: Band did some rehearsing at Brito (I don't remember this at all!)

Saturday 2nd June: St John's Arena, Columbus, Ohio.
Back to what we were all good at doing… Set up everything ready for Sweet who played first (supporting Peter Frampton who was 'Showing everyone the way'.

Monday 4th June: Fort Field Arena, Erie, Pennsylvania.
Sweet set and then Journey. This was a great evening for everyone who was in the building. The prestige of supporting a huge and famous band like Journey was just so exciting and an incredible experience for us all.

Tuesday 5th June: Performing Arts Centre, Buffalo, New York.
Sweet then Journey. This is great music.

Friday 8th June: Palladium, New York, New York.
Sweet, Journey.

Saturday 9th June: Capitol Theatre Passaic, New Jersey.
Sweet, Journey.

Tuesday 12th June: Broome County Arena, Binghampton, New York.
Sweet, Journey. Music to my ears every night. Coach driver drove us through the night to Portland, Maine.

Wednesday 13th June: Wow a day off. Jerry, Nick, Des, Martin and I sunbathed on Orchard Beach. Jerry and I had four rides on a jumbo jet big dipper while they were just testing it. Great stuff. Back to our hotel, swim in the pool, shower then all went to Da Millo's Seafood restaurant.

I had a "Surf and Turf" and a nice few wines. We then all went to The Loft night club; cab back to the hotel, played table pinball for a while and climbed into bed at 1:00am. Now that's energy… And believe me you couldn't be in that industry unless you had energy.

Thursday 14th June: Cumberland Coliseum, Portland, Maine.
Bit more information on this one, A beautiful morning. Trevor and I went for a ride in car north to Freeport Landing Stage, beautiful, reminded me of Canada. Had lobster roll and chocolate milk.

Off to gig, Journey leading again. Great evening had by all, boy that Steve Perry could sing… beautiful voice.

Friday 15th June: Performing Arts Centre, Saratoga, New York.
A nice semi outdoor gig. I remember the audience were great. Wow.

Saturday 16th June: Orpheum Theatre, Boston, Massachusetts.
All went very well. This was a really nice tour.

Sunday 17th June: Columbia, Maryland.
Just slipping a feeling in here: If someone took me to all of these gigs/destinations now, I wonder if I would remember some of them. Fascinating though, eh?

Tuesday 19th June: Civic Centre, Savannah, Georgia.
Something different here! No Journey, but KISS, instead! Another great crowd. The American audiences really know how to enjoy music, even going back to Bill Haley and the Comets.

Thursday 21st June: Mobile, Alabama.
Sweet followed by Blue Öyster Cult. So nice to work with other great bands.

Saturday 23rd June: Sunken Garden Theatre, San Antonio, Texas.
We all thought sometimes that we had travelled further than the Space Shuttle!
    This was an outdoors gig. It was a stiflingly hot day. Fools were the opening act here and Sweet were the headliners.

Sunday 24th June: Manor Downs, Austin, Texas.
(Outdoors) Fools, Sweet and headliners Cheap Trick. A lot of shuffling around of equipment on this gig as you can imagine. Drove until 4:00 a.m. to reach the Corpus Christi Holiday Inn at Emerald Beach.

Monday 25th June: Day off.

Tuesday 26th June: Memorial Coliseum, Corpus Christi, Texas.
Not sure why but Cheap Trick were before Sweet at this gig!

Wednesday 27th June: Civic Centre, Beaumont, Texas.
Back to normal with Cheap Trick closing the show.

Thursday 28th June: Sam Houston Coliseum, Houston, Texas.
With Cheap Trick.

Saturday 30th June: Hirsch Memorial Coliseum, Shreveport, Louisiana.
With Cheap Trick.

Sunday 1st July: Convention Centre Arena, Dallas, Texas.
After lunch the crew walked to the gig. Cheap Trick were doing their sound check.

Sweet played first. We packed our gear up and off the stage. Cheap Trick started their set and about half way through Andy was invited on stage to join them performing The Beatles' 'Day Tripper'. Mick was then invited to join in on their next song. This was such a nice gesture and of course the audience loved it and went crazy.

Monday 2nd July: Lloyd Noble Centre, Norman, Oklahoma
Sweet did their set and then were invited up for a jam again. All great stuff. And this was the last gig of the tour.

Tuesday 3rd July: A long, long day. Crew and the band left for Will Rodgers Airport in Oklahoma City. We got the Braniff 727 flight to New York via Tulsa and Washington! Ugh!

Got cab to TWA terminal at JFK airport. Got 8:00pm Flight 700 to London. All in all, a very boring day. We arrived at Heathrow at 8:40am after a six-hour, five minute flight.

Well, that was another lovely tour to add to the collection. I used to say to myself, "I am seeing the world, whilst hearing the world of music… fabulous."

Monday 9th July: Martin and I went to collect some bits and pieces from Andy's house, whilst he was still in New York. Went to our office to sort a number of things out and finished the day dropping some equipment off at the warehouse.

****

It would appear from my diaries that from now until November was a downtime period to unwind.

****

Monday 12th November: Martin and I went to *Avis* to hire a 3-ton truck to move all of the band's equipment to Shepperton Studios, Stage1. Did two more loads and finished up at 5:30 pm.

Tuesday 13th November: We moved three more truckloads to Shepperton Studios (Andy joined us for lunch). Finished early evening.

Around this time the band set up a business to hire stage equipment out to other bands. The object of this was that everything except guitars and drums could be rented from a great location during any down times. Good thinking!

Wednesday 14th November: Finally finished moving everything to Shepperton Studios.

Thursday 15th November: Jerry, Trevor, Martin and I went to Heathrow airport to collect the remainder of the gear from the USA. Sorry but I am very confused here and don't remember why any equipment was left in the USA. Please forgive me. it was forty-two years ago!

Friday 16th November: Collected few final pieces of gear from airport, after having it cleared through Customs.

Saturday 17th November: Set up some gear at Shepperton for Sweet to have a small rehearsal.

Monday 19th November: Martin and I went to *Avis* again to rent a 3-ton truck to take required equipment to Kingsway Recorders in London. Finished at 10:30pm.

Wednesday 21st November: Went to Shepperton studios to pick up a couple of guitars and then on to Kingsway Recorders.

Friday 23rd November: Martin and I went to Shepperton Studios again. Our Portakabin / container had arrived and had been put in a studio so that when equipment went in there, it would be doubly secure.

In the evening we went back to Kingsway Recorders to see how the recordings were going.

Saturday 24th November: Back to *Avis* to hire a 3-tonner to load all the gear to return it to its 'new home' at Shepperton. Is everyone reading all this realising how fit road crews need to be?

Tuesday 27th November: Jerry and Martin arrived at Kingsway Recorders to load gear and return it to our new home at Shepperton. I stayed on at the studio for a while as the band were doing some mixing and making a wonderful job of it.

Wednesday 28th November: Had a drink with Andy at the pub and then back to the studio.

Thursday 29th November: I picked Andy up and we went to the office and then on to Kingsway. This was a late-night finish… I took Andy home.

Friday 30th November: Picked Andy up and went to the studio. The band had finished two tracks 'Sixties Man' and 'The Lady Needs To Know You'. So we were now finished in the studios so we packed all the equipment up and returned it to Shepperton.

Sunday 2nd December: Martin came over and picked me up. We went to Shepperton Studios to collect some equipment for Andy (he was producing another band called Sussex).

We took the equipment to Kingsway Recorders in London. We got the gear in and stayed and listened for a while. I apologise but I cannot remember the name of the band but they were sounding good.

Tuesday 4th December: We went to Shepperton studios and met Trevor who had got the wood to make the workbench to be able to do repairs on any equipment, ready to start the band's rental service of musical equipment.

Wednesday 5th/Thursday 6th December: We made the workbench... In the afternoon Jerry arrived and fitted all the electrical plug boards to the workbench and cleaned and vacuumed the Portacabin.

Thursday 13th December: Took some more equipment to Kingsway Recorders studio for Andy.

Saturday 15th December: This has absolutely nothing to do with Sweet but I came across it and just had to put it in... On this evening my wife and I went to Hammersmith Odeon to see Cliff Richard in concert. It was excellent but so different to our guys!

Monday 17th December: Trevor, Martin and I went to Kingsway Recorders again, this time to collect equipment from Andy's session with Sussex, who he was helping with their production. (A single 'With A Girl Like You' b/w 'What Can I Say' was released on Mercury in 1980)

In the evening Mick Angus, Brian and I went to Shepperton Studios and had a drink in the bar. They then took me home in Brian's Rolls Royce (black and beautiful).

Wednesday 19th December: My Dad's birthday — bless him. Trevor, Martin and I worked on equipment at Shepperton (soldering, checking, etc etc.)

Friday 21st December: Office party at Handle Artists the band's management company. Had Christmas drinks and all received a Handle jacket. We were now on a break for Christmas.

Thursday 27th December: Martin called to let me know that Mick's wife Pauline, had died last night in a tragic accident at home. This was a tragic end to the year.

POP WIFE DIED OF ASPHYXIA

THE wife of Mick Tucker, drummer with the pop group The Sweet, who was found slumped in the bath at the couple's luxury home, died from asphyxia, it was disclosed today.

Police ruled out any suspicious cirumstances after a post-mortem on 27-year-old Pauline Tucker, who was found by her 30-year-old husband on Thursday at their £150,000 home Troutstream Way, Loudwater, Chorleywood, Hertfordshire.

Tests are still being carried out into what caused the asphyxia, a Rickmansworth police spokesman said. An inquest is expected to be opened at Uxbridge next week.

1980

According to my diaries, January was a month of rest.

Wednesday 6th February: I drove to Gatwick Airport to pick Steve up from a flight from NYC. I had written a song and played it to him in the car on the way to the Sweet office and he said he would like to produce it. Boy, this made my day!

Friday 8th February: David Walker phoned me to say he had got me a record deal with Polydor for the song that I had written.

Monday 11th February: I was told that David Walker had booked Polydor studios for me. Things seemed to be on the up.

Wednesday 13th February: I went to David Walker's office to sign a publishing contract with Handle Music (David's company).

There was a lot of rental of Sweet's equipment out of Shepperton Studios now and we were all keeping up to date with new equipment etc.

Monday 18th February: I had a meeting with David Walker, the band's manager again at 11:00am. He asked me if I would like to see the Polydor Studios in the afternoon. Obviously yes! After lunch I went with David to Polydor Studios and was introduced to their studio engineer David Moore. We had a nice positive chat.

Saturday 23rd February: I had been booked at Polydor Studios to record my song from 2:00pm until 10:00pm but it was changed until the next day.

Sunday 24th February: Polydor studio — Booked from midday until 10:00pm to record my song.

I was an excited Bunny. I played my song which was an instrumental called 'The Clown'. Finished today's work on it at 7:00pm and mixed it until 9:20pm. I put up acoustic guitar on the B-side. Ready to be back at the studios the next day.

Monday 25th February: I was back at the studios and worked on the B-side until 7:00pm. We mixed it (too good for a B-side I thought). We edited the A-side and made acetates of it.

Tuesday 26th February: I went to David Walker's office and played him the recording and he was pleased.

The last few days of the month, and the permanent crew and myself were at Shepperton Studios, renting equipment to various bands, musicians etc.

Tuesday 11th March: My birthday — 33!

Tuesday 18th March: Chipping Norton Studio for me. After collecting the master tape from Polydor, I went home and to bed at 2:30am.

Wednesday 19th March: I worked on my track 'The Clown', again all afternoon and evening until 10:00pm. I did a rough mix of it and got to bed at 1:45am.

Thursday 20th March: Started mixing and finished around 4:00pm including having copies made etc.

Monday 24th March: Went to Shepperton Studios and restrung and cleaned guitars etc. Then had lunch in the Anchor Hotel. Andy arrived and we had drinks and chatted. Went back to the studios and chatted with Andy most of the afternoon and Martin went home. I had drinks in the bar with Andy and he then dropped me home at 9:00pm having discussed everything.

Andy and I often had one-to-one chats about where the band

should go from here, and if I could, I would try and come up with new ideas from a different perspective which I think he appreciated — these were great chats!).

This was all forty-one years ago! Oh my god.

Sunday 30th March: Martin and I met Mick Tucker at Shepperton Studios on our storage level. He played for about an hour trying out new bits for drum solos etc. Mick was the keenest drummer I ever met. He lived for drums and loved every moment of playing, and rehearsing.

Thursday 3rd April: We had a meeting with Tony from Shepperton Studios about needing a little more storage space for all the band's equipment. Went to the Anchor pub for lunch, and then back to the studios and got the okay from Tony, manager of this particular area in the studios.

Tuesday 8th, Wednesday 9th & Thursday 10th April: All of the crew were at Shepperton Studios getting Sweet's equipment to the new larger storage place.

Friday 11th April: A busy, hard day… This is my diary wording: Went to Shepperton studios. Guys from a crane company arrived to lift our Portacabin up to a higher level. It took one and a half hours to get it to the top level. The crew rolled it into its final position. The rest of Sweet's equipment was positioned in rows. Jerry rewired the mains and telephone into the final position. We finished at 7:35pm. Pooped.

Monday 14th April: We put new wheels on the band's flight cases where needed.

Tuesday 15th April: Got my acetate of my instrumental 'The Clown' but it was the old version from Polydor studios. What the fuck!

Wednesday 16th April: At Shepperton Studios and got lots of phone calls asking about Sweet's PA system for hire.

Thursday 17th April: David Walker told me that London Weekend Television loved my track 'The Clown' and were going to use it. Naturally I felt really good about this.

Monday 21st April: Sweet's PA was rented to Led Zeppelin for a rehearsal (good business).

Monday 28th April: went to Shepperton Studios and collected Andy's 8-track Brenell recorder. I took it to Andy's house and had a nice chat.

The first week of June was spent getting even more sorted out at Shepperton Studios with the increasing rental equipment.

Sunday 8th June: David Walker's birthday party. I went to the London office and had food and drinks. Later in the day went home got showered etc. I went in the evening to Neasden Golf Club to David's party. A lot of people from the industry were there Andy and Trevor arrived a little later. got home at 2:00am.

All this period was to do with the band's rental company of musical equipment that Martin and I were working on full time.

Monday 16th June: I have to put this in because it is a sad fact of life that happens to us all... at 3:45am a policeman and a policewoman knocked at the front door of my house in Wraysbury. They gave me and my wife the sad news that totally unexpectedly my dad had died this evening of a heart attack.

So, so sad. He had been behind me all the years I was working with Sweet and he had been very happy to see me enjoying travelling around the world doing something I really loved.

He knew Brian and Mick very well from when they were in my band and my dad was managing us. Needless to say they were very sad at the news.

Monday 30th June: Went to Andy's flat for his birthday party. All the usual people were there. It was an excellent party. I was the last to leave at 4:15am and I was in bed by 5:00am.

The crew went through July working on the band's equipment

rental side and keeping quite busy. But this is not touring! Let's get on the road!

Wednesday 13th August: I went to Wandsworth to Event Studios for a TV filming session. Sweet arrived and did a promotional film.

Friday 29th August: I was at Shepperton Studios with all of Sweet's gear and a guy came and bought Mick Tuckers 8-track Brenell recorder for £2,600. That was a lot of money then.

Monday 15th September: I went to Andy's house to collect his Ampeg amplifier. We listened to some tapes. I took the amplifier to Marcus Studios in Kensington for a rental client. I went onto our office to collect some bits and pieces for Andy. Drove to Andy's house and we chatted I always enjoyed talking with Andy it was always about positive things, ideas, way to do things etc. Steve arrived and we all went to the Anchor pub for lunch.

Thursday 25th September: We painted Mick's wooden/perspex drum riser as there was a client going to rent it. He then cancelled but a good job was done anyway.

Friday 26th September: Went with Martin to Shepperton to sort out studio equipment for the band.

Saturday 27th September: Loaded vans with equipment for the studio with Jerry and Martin. We took the gear to Marcus Studios.

Sunday 28th September: Went to Shepperton to collect more of Sweet's gear and then onto Marcus Studios. Andy and Steve were there.

Monday 29th September: I went to Andy's house to collect a few more pieces for the studio. Martin was at Shepperton collecting the Leslie 950.

Monday 6th October: This month seemed to be quieter than usual for the band, but myself and Jerry and Martin were relatively busy at Shepperton Studios renting out equipment to bands, studios etc.

Sunday 26th October: Martin picked me up and we went to Marcus Studios. Jerry and Sweet were already there. I have no info in my diary as to what they were recording and it is a bit too long ago to remember but when we finished that evening I took Andy and Steve home.

Saturday 1st November: I went to Marcus Studios. The engineer and I went to collect our Yamaha CS80 keyboard from Basing Street Studio.

I went and picked Steve Priest up and we went back to the studio.

When we finished for that day I took Steve home and he gave me the new Kansas tape. this was one of my favourite bands. We still had a crew of three of us at this time working for the band, mainly from Shepperton studios renting out high end musical equipment.

Wednesday 12th November: This will appeal to some of you. I soldered 48 Cannon plugs on to 24 leads. 144 joints.

Tuesday 18th/Wednesday 19th November: Jerry and I were still making up and soldering new leads to always offer exceptional reliable equipment whilst it wasn't being used by Sweet.

This was all actually a very good idea by the band as a band really is better to have a permanent bunch of guys that all think on the same wavelength.

****

Hi everyone – there is more! There are so many bits of information, purchases, repairs, buying, soldering, renting, driving, delivering, travelling by road, by plane, place names, city names. Plus of course the guys and the gigs! Read on…

Sunday 14th December: I went to Heathrow airport to meet Steve Priest from his flight from New York.

Monday 15th December: Went to Shepperton Studios and met Martin and Jerry there. We got rehearsal gear over into Rock City's Nissen Hut and got everything set up for Sweet to have a rehearsal.

Had lunch in the canteen then a drink in the bar with Mick Tucker. The others arrived and they rehearsed until 8:40pm when we all had a couple of drinks in the bar.

Tuesday 16th-Thursday 18th December: Rehearsals continued.

Friday 19th December: Finished rehearsals. The crew broke down the equipment and we got it all back to our area in Shepperton Studios again.

Monday 22nd December: I went to Brian's to check a pair of loudspeakers for him.

Tuesday 23rd December: This was a day when myself and the crew went and collected lots of rentals of their equipment to put away before Christmas.

Thursday 25th December: Christmas Day. A personal piece here... My wife, son and I went to my mum's house on the River Thames near Staines. We all went into my mum's next door neighbours Kay and Arthur's, for a Christmas drink and then back to Mum's for a wonderful Christmas dinner and had our presents, and lovely long chats until we headed home at 10:00pm and clambered into bed at 12:45am.

Friday 26th December: Woke up at 1:15am when Doreen, my mum's next-door neighbour rung me to say that mum was ill and could hardly breathe! I dialled 999 and asked for an ambulance as quickly as possible. We dashed over in the car and the ambulance had already arrived. It turned out she had a bad throat infection. They gave her an injection and penicillin. She was taken to hospital and got checked over and thankfully got taken home again. Phew!

Saturday 27th December: Back to work. I went to Shepperton Studios. Sid, Jerry, Martin and Simon arrived. We all set Sweet's gear up on M stage. Sweet arrived and we did rehearsals until 9:15pm.

Sunday 28th December: Another day of rehearsals. I sang harmonies in three songs. We finished at 9:30pm.

Monday 29th December: Rehearsals again until 8:45pm.

Tuesday 30th December: Rehearsals until 6:30pm.

Wednesday 31st December: Rehearsals until 5:45pm.

1981

Thursday 1st January: I went to Shepperton Studios. Sweet arrived. Big rehearsal and complete run through. We all went to the pub after having a McDonald's and had a drink or two.

Back to the studio and did another complete run through and finished at 9:50pm.

Friday 2nd January: All back to Shepperton Studios to do another full run through for their management team. Ed Leffler from the USA, David Walker and Lindsey Brown from their London office.

Had a break and we all went for a drink and then back to Shepperton to do another complete run through of their set. You can see here how hard everybody has to work in the music business.

Saturday 3rd January: Day of rest for all concerned... Phew!

Sunday 4th January: The Lyceum Theatre in London... 9:00am. I drove to the Lyceum and met the rest of the crew there. We had some help from six Humpers. (Marvellous strong guys that make all this possible). The band arrived at 4:00pm for a sound check which went really well before the two support bands, The Minutes and Dumb Blondes, did their soundchecks.

So we now had a long break, the crowds arrived and filled the Lyceum. The two guest bands did their sets. At 9:45pm Sweet came on to huge applause and played until 11:00pm. They went down great. It was so thrilling to see everyone living every minute.

Friday 9th January: This was an interesting change from usual. I picked Mike Sherwin from Datchet. He was Andy's Aston Martin service guy. We went to Andy's flat, and I then followed them to R.S. Williams (Aston Martin service centre) in Brixton in London.

We had a bacon sandwich and a cup of tea in a café. I then ran Mike back to Datchet. Went to Shepperton Studios to work on checking equipment over etc.

The next two weeks myself and Martin were quite busy with equipment rental and servicing stuff for the Sweet guys. The Shepperton Studios equipment rental idea of those was a great idea. It meant there was a constant income coming in and importantly it meant that they kept a road crew for a very long time.

Thursday 5th February: Loaded the Yamaha CS80 big electronic keyboard onto Martin's van and took it to Polydor Studios. He was producing a band named Heroes there.

Tuesday 10th February: Went to Brian's house to drop a few items off from the studios for him, and then went on to Shepperton and mended Andy's TEAC four track recorder which needed a new micro switch.

Wednesday 18th February: Went to Chandlers Guitars to get a few replacement parts for one of Andy's guitars.

Thursday 19th February: Finished working on Andy's guitar.

Wednesday 25th February: Moved equipment at Shepperton across to another unit for the band to do rehearsals. Martin arrived with Steve from the airport. Rehearsals through until 7:00pm.

Friday 27th February: More rehearsals — just another day at the office!

Monday 2nd, Tuesday 3rd & Wednesday 4th March: These three days were full of excitement as we were all hyped up, ready for the first gig of the tour at Newcastle. On the 4th all the gear and equipment was loaded into a big articulated truck for its journey up to Newcastle.

Thursday 5th March: My breakfast and packing done, I got a train to Waterloo and met the others there. We drove to Newcastle in a

VW LT crew bus, once there we checked into the Centre Hotel for the night.

Friday 6th March: City Hall, Newcastle.
UK tour starts. Great to be on the road again.

Saturday 7th March: Rock City, Nottingham.
The Sweet set wasn't until 11:30pm.

The new Sweet trio (left to right): Andy Scott, Steve Priest and Mick Twicker.

Sweet and sour

by BARBARA DAY

THE SWEET smell of success turned sour for drummer Mick Tucker when he realised the days of teenybop glam rock had to end in the mid-Seventies.

He was one of the founder members of Sweet, the band that turned out 14 hit singles inside three years and opened their new British tour at Newcastle's City Hall last night.

Hits like 'Ballroom Blitz', 'Wig Wam Bam' and 'Little Willie' turned the four struggling musicians into pop heroes with more than a little help from the lucrative Nicky Chinn-Mike Chapman hit factory.

"But we found ourselves on a merry-go-round which meant we were only as good as our next single. As one song started to come down the charts we would have already recorded the follow-up, knowing it was going to make the top three," said Mick.

"We could have gone on working with Chinn and Chapman and probably had another dozen hits and I'm sure it would have continued to be quite lucrative.

"But there comes a point where you have to get off that merry-go-round if you believe in yourselves as musicians, as artistes and as an act.

The lads had already earned some critical acclaim for their own compositions which were recorded as B-sides on the successful singles. And the turning point came with 'Fox on the Run'. They wrote, recorded and produced it themselves and it turned out to be their biggest seller.

The tour which opened in Newcastle last night was their first appearance in Britain for more than three years, so I asked Mick what had happened to Sweet since those heady days of teenybop glory ended.

"We've been touring the rest of Europe, Japan, Australia and America. It was so different, because in England people can only relate to seeing you on 'Top of the Pops' and you can only pull crowds if your single is in the charts.

"The biggest venue we played was a 30,000-seater in Rhode Island and we toured with Bob Seeger for six weeks. In America, you could stay on the road for years and not reach saturation point, but we could only take so much and we've spent about four months out of each of the last five years touring there.

"At one stage we came off the road to record for about 18 months. And we've toured places like New Zealand, Scandinavia and Germany quite a lot.

"The fans in Japan, for instance, are amazing. They love anything that's English, for a start. There were thousands of people at every airport and it was a bit embarrassing because we'd long since dropped the teenybop band image.

"The gigs in Tokyo were sell-outs and the audiences are pretty well clued-up on rock acts. It's weird, though, because they sit there really quiet before you come on but once you actually get on stage they're going crazy enjoying themselves."

Renewed chart success came in the late seventies with yet another hit single, 'Love is Like Oxygen'. Then Sweet's blond lead singer, Brian Connolly, left, leaving Mick to work in a threesome with guitarist Andy Scott and bassist Steve Priest.

Now they've just released a new album called 'Water's Edge', from which a single has yet to be chosen.

Looking back, 33 year old Mick reckons that risking a break with him and Chapman and ditching the old glam rock label has paid off. He said: "The worst thing in the world is not having a reason to want to work. It's everyone's dream to make a mint, but I've done it and I can tell you, like a hungry boxer who's made it, you've got nothing left to fight for."

Sweet take comeback trail West

THE START of the 1980's has seen almost as many comebacks as new faces with old friends like Slade, Gary Glitter and the heavy metal veterans making an impact once more.

Latest comeback hopefuls are Sweet, formed 13 years ago and led to fame by the then struggling songwriter Mike Chapman and his partner Nicky Chinn. Chapman is Blondie's producer these days.

Sweet are now embarking on their first British tour for more than three years and it calls at the Bath Pavilion next Saturday.

Sweet are now a trio of original members Steve Priest, Andy Scott and Mick Tucker since singer Brian Connolly's departure two years ago.

Steve Priest said: "We are now doing the sort of music we'd planned to play when we started; three piece rock 'n' roll with a bit of subtlety."

Tuesday 10th March: Top Rank, Cardiff.
Got all the equipment in down two flights of steps. Can you imagine? the support band and then the Sweet set. A good audience and it worked out really well.

Wednesday 11th March: Unity Hall, Wakefield.
My birthday (again) age 34. Support band were the same as the previous night called the Steve Linton Band, who played their set, and then Sweet came on and did a great set.

Thursday 12th March: Royal Theatre, Liverpool.
We all left Wakefield and drove to Liverpool. Got all the gear set up. The support band played. Sorry guys didn't write your name down. A great audience. Drove back to London.

Friday 13th March: Queen Mary College, London.
Good support band and then Sweet went on and did their stuff. A good gig.

Saturday 14th March: Pavilion, Bath.
Our truck and driver were four hours late because of a puncture. This was always a nightmare if it happened with having so much equipment to set up. Did sound check and went for a curry afterwards. The support band called The Points, did their set and then Sweet did another of their really great sets. The audience really loved them.

A well-deserved break for a few days.

Thursday 19th March: Lancaster University.
Support band did their set and Sweet also did an excellent set.

Friday 20th March: Glasgow University.
This was one of the 'lousy get ins' which also makes the day longer… Sweet on stage at midnight. Good set as always. We left all the equipment until the morning to reload the truck (I can't remember ever doing that before). The gig was the last of the tour.

Thursday 26th March: We, the crew were back at Shepperton Studios. Andy came and was interviewed by Max Kay from *International Musician*.

****

October-December

Well, from April through until now, there were no tours, lots of thinking which way to head forward for the band.

Martin and I continued on with the rental business until the end of 1981 while the band had an extended quieter time, writing new songs and having a well-deserved break and relaxing period.

You have to do this to give your brain and body a time to unwind, so that you can, when you are totally relaxed and feel ready to go. You have lots of new ideas in your head and a lot of exciting thoughts.

1982

January: Extremely quiet...

Friday 5th February: I loaded some gear for Andy from my mother's big garage, which was now where a lot of the gear was being kept for easier availability. And only a few moments from my house.

I went to Lou Austin's to pick him up and we went to Lingfield to the truck mobile recording studio. Andy arrived. He started putting a track down with Lou on a song called 'Gotta See Jane'.

Friday 26th February: Around this time my wife and I were starting a video film rental company in Egham in Surrey, *Square Eyes*. Lots of movies on lots of racks in lots of space. Took off great from day one...

March: Just a few odd little jobs through this month, as the band, it would seem now had disbanded. I am not absolutely sure of this but of course a million and one things happened and they came back doing amazing tours and concerts all over again but with Andy and new members.

The future was left for all to see what happened.

While musical differences was the reason given by their manager David Walker, clearly each of the band members had a lot going on in their personal lives and it seemed to be the end of an era. However, I think the crew were all secretly hoping that something more would evolve or eventually come together with the original four…

****

Sweet temptations

FANCY making a fast million dollars ? Brian Connolly, who used to lead The Sweet, reckons that is what a new group in the same mould stands to earn.

"There is a big gap ready to be filled for a pop group like The Sweet," he says. "If somebody came along with the right image I reckon they could easily make a million dollars."

Brian left The Sweet in 1979 after nine years to produce other bands and he has just finished his first solo single.

"Yeah, I miss being in a band," he says. "That's why I am back. I don't miss the glamour and all the other stuff, I just miss playing."

COMEBACK: Connolly

But hey! As we all know they all loved what they did and Steve moved permanently to the USA and formed a great outfit called Sweet. Andy did amicably, as I understand it, the same thing in England and had some great line-ups over the future years.

I'm writing this now February the 27th 2021 thinking... "didn't they do well and "aren't they doing well." I just love 'Still Got The Rock', a great song and an absolutely fantastic recording. Best of luck guys.

So, my movements from 1982 onwards… Some I have already written about and this will only be the highlights but a lot of them.

Tributes flood in for glam rock singer

The pop world last night paid tribute to Brian Connolly, the lead singer of 1970s glam rock band The Sweet, who died yesterday, aged 52.

"You never lost your touch, mate," said Don Powell and Dave Hill of Slade.

They added: "We had a lot of laughs during the 1970s and we have just recently made contact again doing concerts together in Europe.

"To us, your records always sounded brilliant, and that's our memory of you, dear Brian."

Suzi Quatro, from the same Chinn and Chapman stable as The Sweet, said: "Their records still stand up today. Nobody says: 'Who?' and thank God, nobody says it about mine either.

"Brian was a nice man, very easy to talk to, but he did live the rock and roll lifestyle.

Connolly, whose hits included *Blockbuster, Ballroom Blitz* and *Wig Wam Bam*, died of renal failure in hospital in Slough with his friends and family around him. He had a string of heart-attacks, which started in 1981 after years of rock 'n' roll excess.

He suffered the last in January this year, discharged himself from hospital after a week, but was re-admitted a week later.

At the height of their fame The Sweet enjoyed hits both in Britain and in America, and sold 50 million records worldwide.

Pop fame: The Sweet enjoyed success on both sides of the Atlantic, with singer Brian Connolly, far right.

Connolly left in 1979, but his solo career was dogged by ill health.

However, as late as last year he was playing live, re-creating The Sweet's hits throughout Europe.

Friend and colleague Jamie Doran said yesterday: "Connolly was a one-off: A cantankerous, charismatic performer and a survivor."

He was a talented musician who planned to work on some film scores for Doran's company Atlantic Celtic Films, Mr Doran said. Connolly leaves a girlfriend, Jean, their two-year-old son Brian, and two daughters Nicola, 22, and Michelle, 19, by his marriage to Marilyn.

His half brother was Mark McManus, the actor who played popular Scottish detective *Taggart* and who also died of drink-related problems, in 1994.

Although brought up together, they did not hear they were actually blood relatives until they were adults.

Brian Connolly

Lead singer of the 'glam rock' band Sweet who was a British teen icon in the 1970s

BRIAN CONNOLLY, who has died aged 52, was the lead singer with the 1970s "glam rock" band Sweet.

In flares, glitter and sequins, Sweet epitomised a moment in the early 1970s when tongue-in-cheek camp overtook almost all rivals in the charts. Their several No 2 singles were only held off from the top of the charts by such songs as Dawn's *Tie A Yellow Ribbon*, the Bay City Rollers' *Bye Bye Baby*, and Middle of the Road's *Chirpy Chirpy Cheep Cheep*.

Nevertheless, with songs such as *Little Willy*, *Blockbuster* and *Ballroom Blitz*, Sweet sold 50 million records between 1971 and 1979. Connolly, with blonde feather-cut locks and mandatory glam rock eye make-up, was a full-blown teen icon.

The bubble burst with the arrival of punk, and Connolly's career, after he left the group in 1979, was a series of faltering come-backs marred by ill-health after years of excess. As the band's bass player later put it, "We were drinking too much and taking too many drugs — which seemed like a good idea at the time — but it seemed to affect Brian more than anyone else."

Brian Connolly was born on Oct 5 1944 at Hamilton, Scotland. His family moved to Middlesex when he was 12, and at 18 he found out that he was adopted. His half-brother was the actor Mark McManus, who later played Taggart in the television series.

When he was 17 Connolly replaced Ian Gillan (who later found fame with Deep Purple) as the singer with Wainwright's Gentlemen, a small-time soul band from Harrow.

Two years later he and the band's drummer, Mick Tucker, formed Sweetshop, with Steve Priest on bass and Frank Torpey on guitar. After shorten-

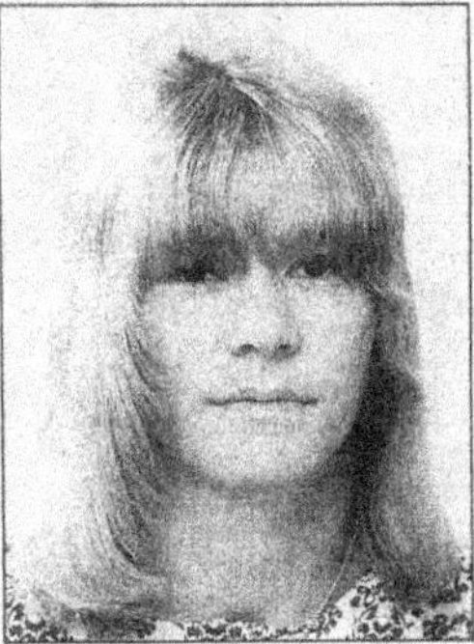

Connolly: flamboyant image

ing the name to Sweet they released four singles on Fontana and EMI.

But the singles flopped and EMI dropped the band. A new guitarist, Andy Scott, was drafted in, and in 1971 they signed a recording deal with RCA, and were introduced to the writing partnership of Nicky Chinn and Mike Chapman. The "Chinnichap" writing team was to be the making of the band. The first single, *Funny Funny*, released in May that year, reached No 13, and in July *Co-Co* made No 2.

A string of hits followed, each one a perfect example of bubblegum glam rock. *Little Willy* and *Wig Wam Bam* both made No 4 on the charts, while in January 1973 *Blockbuster*, using one of the most familiar riffs in rock music (the same one as in David Bowie's *The Gene Genie*, which sat at No 2) gave them their first and only British No 1.

It was followed by *Hellraiser*, *Ballroom Blitz* — which begins with the sound of a wailing siren — and *Teenage Rampage*, each one reaching No 2 in Britain. *Teenage Rampage* was kept from the No 1 position by Mud's *Tiger Feet*, another archetypal song of that era, also written by Chinnichap. Meanwhile, *Little Willy* was No 3 in America and sold more than a million copies.

By this time, Sweet were regulars on *Top of the Pops* and had plunged wholeheartedly into a glam rock image. Each single marked ever more outrageous and flamboyant costumes, with higher platform boots, more make-up and wilder glitter. In Belgium the band were taken to court for using an allegedly pornographic film clip at a concert, while in Britain they were banned from Mecca dancehalls for what was considered an overtly sexual stage act.

More singles appeared in 1974 and 1975 to good reception, and a three-month American tour was a sell-out. But in December 1974 the band split from Chinn and Chapman to rely on their own songs, but their own brand of melodic rock fell between the two markets of the teenyboppers and the more mature rock fans. By 1979 Sweet was disintegrating.

In 1981 Connolly had a series of heart attacks from which he never fully recovered. Various reincarnations of Sweet appeared over the next decade, though none to the band's previous acclaim.

Brian Connolly is survived by his former wife Marilyn, and by two daughters and a son.

Mick Tucker

Drummer with 1970s glam-rock band The Sweet

MICK TUCKER, who has died aged 54, was the drummer with The Sweet, the glam rock band that came to prominence in the early 1970s; if their music was never sensational, their appearance and their antics, both on and off-stage, afforded ample compensation for their fans.

By 1973 – the year in which they were at the height of their popularity – their behaviour on stage had led some clubs in Britain to ban them from appearing, and they were already well down the road to excess. Tucker once recalled spending three days in a German hotel with The Who during which time "we drank constantly and had nothing to eat – I wasn't feeling too good".

Michael Thomas Tucker was born on July 17 1947 at Harlesden, north-west London. By the age of 19 he had embarked on a career in pop music, playing around pubs and clubs in a band called Wainwright's Gentlemen. According to the fashion of the day, they mixed Motown with R & B, adding a dash of psychedelia.

In 1968 Tucker and the vocalist, Brian Connolly, broke away to form Sweet-

Tucker: the one-handed twirl

shop, with Steve Priest on bass and Frank Torpey on guitar. Four unsuccessful singles later Torpey was replaced by Andy Scott; the new line-up, now called The Sweet, signed up to RCA and success was around the corner.

At RCA, The Sweet were fortunate to have the assistance of the writing partnership of Nicky Chinn and Mike Chapman, who provided them with "bubblegum" pop anthems such as *Funny Funny* (1971), *Co-Co* (1971), and *Poppa Joe* (1972).

The band's only No 1 came in 1973 with *Blockbuster*, but other Top 10 hits included *Hell Raiser* (1973) and *Teenage Rampage* (1974); there was also *Ballroom Blitz* (1973), which reached a new audience when it featured in the film *Wayne's World* in 1992.

From an early stage, however, The Sweet aimed to appeal beyond the tennyboppers who provided their early fan base, recording hard-rock numbers on the B-sides of their hit singles. In performance, these songs gave Tucker the opportunity to show off his characteristic drum rolls and one-handed twirl of the drum sticks.

By 1974 The Sweet's heyday was over, and in 1979 Connolly left to pursue a solo career. The band broke up in the early 1980s, although there were occasional attempts to reform.

Tucker had suffered from leukaemia for the past five years. His wife Janet and their 22-year-old daughter were at his bedside when he died.

2003

Tuesday 25th February: My wife Tina and I moved to Truckee near Lake Tahoe California USA. We had already purchased a vacation home which we used to use three times a year for three weeks each time. Heading back to England got harder and harder every time, as we love the walks in the spring, the walks and boating in the summer, and the skiing in the winter.

So we took the plunge and moved there permanently. After a while we decided to start a second home care business. There was an immediate build-up of clients and of staff. Very hard work, but also satisfying. Skiing at Squaw Valley Lake Tahoe was $75 a day but for residents $395 for a season, a no brainer.

By 2008 I wanted to slow down a bit so had a few extra part time staff and spent more of my spare time relaxing. This was a time in life when we thought what do we want to do from here? We parted from the business and let life slow down a little and enjoyed every moment.

2011

We spoke to a friend who we met on a vacation to Mexico and asked him where he was now living. His name was Grant and his immediate words to us were come and live in Merida in the Yucatan. I said to him "the Yucatan", where is that? He said to me, "I will show you where it is".

So, I got my atlas and he said to me, "see if you can find it?" No hope, He said go right to the bottom of Mexico and turn back up the huge peninsula. I did, and there it was. I love maps and have looked at maps all my life and had never come across this place, as most people haven't!

So... How about this! We sold our house in Lake Tahoe, got our belongings shifted and got on a plane in Reno, Nevada with our dog Mr. Frodo, changed planes at Houston, Texas and onward to Manuel Crescencio Rejon International Airport in Merida, Yucatan, Mexico. It was quite surreal actually. What an amazing change in lifestyle coming up.

Grant took us from the airport, around the huge ring road off Merida, and then the thirty minutes to the beach home we had rented.

We got there, it was lovely and just one row back from the beach (we went to a supermarket on the way to stock up) unloaded everything, checked out the swimming pool and said a very, very big thank you to Grant.

Unpacked cases, snack, bedtime. Totally pooped...

Well... The following morning we had a lovely lie in and had breakfast and a nice cup of English tea sitting by our swimming pool. This was going to be the start of a new relaxing phase in our lives, or so we thought. This was going to be house number one.

I decided that relaxing for a while was the way to go which I did, but it wasn't long before I got the bug to start doing something again. When you open your eyes every morning this place pretty much tells you the direction to take…… Photography. I was ready to go.

Before you read on you should grab an atlas and go to the Mexico pages, and right at the bottom of Mexico, swing right and northwards and you will be in the state of Yucatan which is a huge peninsula on the Gulf of Mexico, the capital being the Colonial City of Merida which is absolutely beautiful and just thirty-five minutes from the ocean.

Strangely enough, not many people know that it is changing fast with many, many expats arriving all the time, mainly from Canada and the USA but that is now changing and people are starting to arrive from everywhere.

Not surprising really, the ocean is always warm, beautiful sand beaches, hundreds of vacation homes owned by people living in the city of Merida but more people are now making the beach their permanent residence.

There was not a lot to do but relax. Progresso the main town has most things you need and the supermarkets have improved beyond belief. The thing is, it is only a thirty-five minute drive back to Merida on a super wide dual modern highway. The beach homes tend to nearly all be used in July and August, often full time with perhaps wives and children during the week, with the husbands arriving on Friday evenings, but of course, many retirees spend most of their time here at the beautiful beach homes.

After the end of August many are still not empty as the owners have permanent caretakers, or many are rented out during the off season.

Enough. I'm here writing this and would rather be overlooking the ocean and doing it. But seriously wherever I am I will never forget how beautiful life can be if you can make it that way. We moved to the outskirts of the city but only fifteen minutes to the centre. So it was time, after two years at the beach, to move nearer to the city.

We actually rented part of a lovely home outside the city, because it was quiet and peaceful and just outside of a small town. It was a friend's grandmother Dodi who rented to us, she was a really lovely lady.

From this location we could drive into the city of Merida in which we did many times to just look in awe at some other most beautiful buildings, churches etc. And so many bars and restaurants. I can only describe it all as absolutely fascinating, so this made us realise that we could get even closer to the city and still not feel like you were in a city.

So we were recommended to a nice young lady realtor who showed us about six houses and one of them just stood out above the rest. It was halfway down a quiet street with a small front and rear outdoor space and three bedrooms. The house location made it a 'yes' without looking any further. It really was a great location.

I have taken so many beautiful photographs here, along with amazing pictures in Lake Tahoe, California and other areas in the USA and the world.

I soon realised I can't pretend to myself that I am a retiree. So I decided to rent a small commercial property just five minutes from my house in a very small mall by the main road into Merida. There were about nine businesses, from hair salons to big print stores, restaurant etc. I was right next to an Aeromexico ticket office which was closest to the main road.

I got it all fitted out myself to be able to show my photographic art and other bits and pieces that fitted in well to give it a trendy homely look. Bought a nice chair, nice desk and took Mr. Frodo with me every day. Turned on the AC unit and hey presto I was ready to roll.

It was not as busy as I had hoped and after about a year I thought I'm off. I will go and sell my photographic art on my own. Number one, with no rent and two, whenever I wanted another life change. I can honestly say I don't like being bored after such a frenetic life with Sweet. Dictionary says of frenetic — fast and energetic in a rather wild and uncontrolled way.

'I must be frenetic'.

So I started taking huge amounts of photographs at the beach which is just half an hour from Merida. Boats, wildlife, flamingos and even some very unusual photographs by looking deeper into the stuff that you don't normally see. In the city there are some amazing beautiful colonial doors. Beautiful designs, beautiful unique metal work, and usually more than one colour.

At the little, and the large harbour there are some amazingly eye-catching old boats in wild colours, loads of missing paint etc but very photogenic.

Beautiful flamingos and other airborne creatures are abundant. I felt really honoured to not just be amongst all this and seeing it but capturing so much on my beloved Canon camera.

To this day I still go out on photo shoots and see new different things every time, and I love it. My e-mail is artgandi@gmail.com you are welcome to send me your comments.

The Sweet musician dead

A co-founder of the 1970s British glam rock band The Sweet has died. Steve Priest was 72. The bass player and singer's longtime bandmate, Andy Scott, confirmed the news Thursday on Facebook. The Sweet became famous thanks to hits like Ballroom Blitz and Blockbuster before disbanding in 1982.

Signing Off... 2023

Well, who could have even thought that the band would still be out there performing so many years later.

It is with deep, deep sadness that three great guys actually went so early in life, but rest assured I saw, and heard them having a most wonderful time for a lot of years and giving their all, to give us such wonderful music all through those years.

We will never forget them.

I am proud, very, very proud of Andy…, still out there, still with a fantastic line up of guys creating such amazing music all the time. Sweet will definitely be there in the history books.

Thank you for reading my book and enjoying the magic of it all like I did.

Boys will be boys, Sweet will be Sweet… And were!

There was nothing like them, and never will be.

ROCK ON, ROCK ON, ROCK ON